LEFTOVERS

Other Books by Kathy Gunst:

■ ■ ■ ■ ■ ■ ■ ■ ■ ■ ■ ■ ■ ■ ■ ■ ■ ■

Condiments

The Great New England Food Guide

Kathy Gunst

LEFTOVERS

200 Recipes
*50 Simple Master Preparations
and
150 Delicious Variations
for the Second Time Around*

HarperPerennial
A Division of HarperCollinsPublishers

FIRST EDITION

Designed by C. Linda Dingler

Library of Congress Cataloging-in-Publication Data

Gunst, Kathy.
    Leftovers / Kathy Gunst.—1st ed.
        p.   cm.
    ISBN 0-06-055296-4
    ISBN 0-06-096863-X (pbk.)
    1. Cookery (Leftovers) I. Title.
TX652.G86   1990b
641.5′52—dc20   90-4464

91 92 93 94 95 CG/RRD 10 9 8 7 6 5 4 3 2 1
91 92 93 94 95 CG/RRD 10 9 8 7 6 5 4 3 2   (pbk.)

For John and Maya
who encourage me, inspire me,
and keep our kitchen a festive,
warm, and loving place

CONTENTS

ACKNOWLEDGMENTS

This book would never have been possible had it not been for the encouragement, support, and love of many people.

Thank you to my editor, Susan Friedland, who thought up the idea for this book in the first place and who convinced me that a book about leftovers would, indeed, be a worthwhile one.

As always, my agent, Robert Cornfield, was full of inspiration and good advice.

To Deirdre Davis for her thorough editing of these recipes, and to all the cooks who contributed their favorite leftover recipes, thank you.

Thank you to my parents, Nancy and Lee Gunst, for their never-ending supply of love and support. And to my mother-in-law, Nancy Rudolph for her love and good recipes.

To my dear friend Karen Frillmann, for helping me get through the hard times and showing me how to appreciate the good ones.

And to Maya, my daughter, for her beauty and enormous appetite. It's a joy to cook for you. And finally to my husband, John Rudolph. This book is as much yours as it is mine.

INTRODUCTION

I did not grow up in a home where leftovers were ingeniously put to use. Whatever we didn't eat was often thrown out; or else it reappeared a few days later hiding beneath a sauce made from canned gravy. The most famous leftover dish in my family was the Tuesday night special: Mom's spaghetti casserole. This was Monday night's spaghetti and meatball dinner reheated in the oven until the meatballs achieved the consistency of leather.

Leftovers were boring, unappetizing food.

Then, on my first visit to France, I learned that it didn't have to be this way. I was in my early twenties, spending a week with a Parisian family. My hosts, like my own family, clearly could afford to eat whatever they wanted. They didn't need to save food in order to stretch their resources. But I watched in amazement as every scrap of food was not only saved, but also reused in imaginative ways. Peelings from carrots and leeks went into the stockpot. The hard, stale ends of crusty baguettes were saved for making bread crumbs and thickening soups. Bits and pieces of cooked fish were transformed into a luscious stew, laden with garlic and fresh vegetables.

There was a feeling in that home that food was precious. And for me, the most miraculous part of all was that, over the course of my stay, leftover foods were used to make meals that were every bit as delicious as the celebration dinner we had the evening I arrived.

Of course many professional chefs acknowledge that truly good cooks are distinguished by their ability to create meals out of whatever ingredients happen to be available—including leftovers.

My French-born friend Jean Ames, a wonderful cook who has lived in Oaxaca, Mexico, for many years, tells a story illustrating this point. "When my cousin Renée hires a cook, she never asks, 'How would you prepare a *Civet de Lapin*?' but 'What would you do with a cooked chicken wing, a pickle, and two potatoes?' My answer," says Ames, "would be to take the skin off the wing and give it to the cat. I would mince the meat and moisten it with heavy cream, a few drops of Cognac, and season it discreetly with a pinch of nutmeg. I'd make a puree of potatoes, make a pretty shell with the puree, and fill the hollow with my chicken cream. I'd sprinkle on melted butter, put it in the oven, and while it's delicately browning, I'd eat the pickle."

Another friend, Ken Hom, chef, cooking teacher, and host of a Chinese cooking show on PBS, says, "Cooking with leftovers is the true test for a cook. It jars your thinking, because it's not a prescribed method of cooking. It forces you to use your instincts and that's what cooking is all about."

While I was writing this book I spoke with dozens of friends and chefs, and every one of them had a story to tell about leftovers. Many people recalled creating excellent dishes after scouring the contents of the refrigerator on a cold, snowy night, or while at a vacation house miles from the nearest supermarket.

"We rented a house in the woods one summer," a friend told me. "The rain started and the dirt road turned to mush. All we had left in our cooler was a few cooked green beans, a piece of cooked chicken, the end of a hunk of cheese, and four eggs. We made the most incredible omelette you've ever eaten. The truth is that I never would have made a chicken, green bean, and cheese omelette at home, but now it's one of my favorites."

Some of the world's great cuisines rely on previously cooked foods. In China and throughout much of Asia, where ovens are still a rarity in most homes, roast chicken and duck and barbecued pork bought at the local market have long been an essential part of everyday cooking. In a wok set over a gas or charcoal burner, a Chinese cook stir-fries these cooked meats and poultry along with fresh vegetables and seasonings and has a complete meal in a matter of minutes.

Think of such Mexican dishes as tacos and enchiladas, where cooked beef, chicken, or pork are combined with fresh vegetables, cheese, and herbs in a cornmeal or wheat shell. French dishes like cassoulet and crêpes use previously cooked foods, as do such American classics as corned beef hash, fish cakes, chicken pot pie, and vegetable fritters.

The aim of this book is to open your mind to the many creative possibilities offered by leftovers. And let's face it, we all have refrigerators full of leftovers—the remnants of Saturday night's roast beef dinner wrapped in foil, Tuesday's pasta, Friday's fish, Sunday's Chinese takeout.

With just a little imagination you can turn those leftovers into terrific meals. But the first step is to stop thinking of leftovers as "old food." The half a cooked chicken hiding in the back of your refrigerator doesn't look quite as appealing as it did when it came out of the oven two days ago, glistening and golden brown, or when you picked it up from your neighborhood deli. But it's still perfectly fine for putting together several meals in very little time because the main ingredient has already been cooked.

Tonight you can make Chicken Salad with Curried Walnuts, Oranges, and Scallions. Tomorrow the bones and carcass can be used to prepare a simple stock, and the next day you can put together a Greek-Style Chicken-Lemon-Rice Soup.

This book emphasizes quick and simple recipes that make the most of leftover foods, supplementing them with fresh vegetables, herbs, and easy-to-prepare sauces. There are also some more elaborate recipes for those who have the time and energy. Those of you who rely on a microwave oven to reheat your leftovers will soon notice that there is no further mention of the machine in this book. I know they save time, but, archaic as it may sound, I don't own one.

I have borrowed and adapted recipes from all over the world—exotic and familiar. I have also been greatly inspired by Michael Field's book *Culinary Classics & Improvisations* (Alfred A. Knopf, 1965)—the only other worthwhile book I know of that's devoted solely to the subject of leftovers. Field's elegant and intelligent book elevated to great status the idea of using leftovers to create exciting new dishes. His is a tradition I aimed to continue with this book.

The chapters in this book are divided according to food type—poultry, beef, pasta, vegetables, bread, and so forth. Each chapter begins with at least one Master Recipe that explains the basic technique for cooking that type of food from scratch (such as Roast Turkey with Oyster-Herb Stuffing, Veal Braised in Its Own Juices, or Grilled Steak with Provençal Herbs). The Master Recipes are then followed by dozens of leftover innovations.

My hope is that you will discover, as I have, that properly prepared dishes made with leftovers can be better than the original meal. You may find yourself roasting an entire leg of lamb, not just because it makes an elegant meal, but also because the next day you can make Middle Eastern Lamb Sandwiches using pita bread or a Chinese Lamb Hot Pot. Your view of leftovers is about to change.

Kathy Gunst
South Berwick, Maine

September 1990

LEFTOVERS

THE LEFTOVER PANTRY

One big advantage to using leftovers is that they significantly cut down the time it takes to prepare a meal. Often in a matter of minutes you can make a dish that features the flavors and textures of foods that initially take much longer to cook. In other words, you get roast beef without the roasting time.

But to take full advantage of the time savings, and the delicious flavors of leftover foods, you need to do a little advance planning. A well-stocked pantry is the key.

What follows is a list of the basic ingredients—condiments, herbs, spices, bottled sauces, wines, nuts, pasta, canned goods—that you should try to have on hand. Although this list is long, many of the items are quite small and can be stored for a long time. Keep them on a back shelf or in the deepest recesses of your refrigerator or freezer until you need them. This list is also meant to familiarize you with some of the ingredients used throughout the book.

BUTTER

I cook with unsalted butter, because it seems to be fresher than salted butter, and who needs the added sodium? I usually keep a stick or two in the refrigerator for immediate use, as well as several sticks in the freezer.

CANNED AND BOTTLED FOODS

Beans, such as canned *cannellini beans (white kidney beans)*, *chickpeas*, and *red kidney beans*, come in handy for a quick sauté, stew, or casserole. Any unused beans should be removed from the can, stored in a glass or plastic jar, and refrigerated until ready to use. Always drain the liquid from the beans and rinse before using.

Capers are the buds of the caper plant (or shrub) that have been pickled in vinegar or dried and packed in salt. They add a tart flavor to salads, cold and hot sauces, stews, and casseroles. Unless otherwise indicated, capers pickled in vinegar should be drained before using. Once they are opened, I like to cover the top of the capers with a tablespoon or two of olive oil to seal in the flavors. Refrigerated, capers will keep for months.

Chutney is a thick, sweet, and sour sauce spiked with chile, garlic, and ginger that originated in India and is an essential ingredient in that cuisine. Although chutneys are made from a wide variety of fruits and vegetables, the most common commercially available variety is made from mangoes. It is delicious served with curries, and added to salads and vinaigrettes. Once opened, chutney should be refrigerated, and will keep for months.

Cornichons are small French-style pickled gherkin cucumbers. They're delicious chopped into vinaigrettes and sauces and served with cold meats, fish, salads, or pâtés; keep refrigerated.

Horseradish adds a pungent flavor to sauces, cold meats, poultry, fish, salads, vinaigrettes. Commercial white horseradish is simply grated horseradish, vinegar, and salt. Red horseradish is a combination of grated horseradish and cooked beets—it is slightly sweeter and less pungent than the white variety. Once opened, bottled horseradish stays sharp and fresh in the refrigerator for only about two weeks.

Mayonnaise, an egg-and-oil-based sauce, is easy to make at home, but there are times when commercial mayonnaise comes in handy for mixing with chicken and turkey salads or adding to sauces. Once opened, mayonnaise must be refrigerated, where it will keep for months.

Mustard is used in all sorts of recipes in this book—sauces, vinaigrettes, stews, and casseroles. One of the most versatile is the strong, creamy Dijon-style mustard. Grainy mustards, in which some of the seeds are left whole or only partially ground, are also excellent for their flavor and texture. Mustard will stay fresh in the refrigerator for several months before going "flat."

Pimiento is the Spanish word for pepper. In this country pimiento generally refers to those red peppers that have been roasted, seeded, and peeled, then preserved in oil or water. Their soft texture and subtly sweet flavor are pleasant in salads, stews, pizza, meat, poultry, and seafood and antipasto platters. If necessary, they can be substituted for freshly roasted red peppers, but you won't get the same texture and fresh, sweet taste. Once the jar has been opened, spoon a tablespoon of olive oil over the pimientos to seal in the flavors; store in the refrigerator.

Salsa is a mixture of chopped (and often pureed) tomatoes, chile peppers, sweet peppers, onions, and spices. There are now many good bottled salsas on the market; see the recipe for homemade salsa on page 237. Use it with tacos and tortillas, grilled meats, poultry, and fish, and add it to other sauces. Salsa will stay fresh in the refrigerator for several weeks.

Tabasco is a blend of chile peppers, salt, and vinegar aged into a fiery hot, thin red sauce. A dash adds tremendous flavor to soups, stews, and sauces. Tabasco is the brand name of a specific sauce made in Louisiana; I prefer it to almost all other types of liquid hot pepper sauce because of its full flavor and fiery punch. Tabasco will stay fresh for several months and need not be refrigerated; store it in a cool, dark spot.

Tahini (also called sesame paste) is made by grinding roasted, hulled sesame seeds into a thick paste similar to unhomogenized peanut butter. Most tahini is light brown in color, with a rich, subtle flavor and smooth texture. It adds a nutty taste to sauces, vinaigrettes, and dips. Tahini will stay fresh, refrigerated, for several months. If it gets too thick, simply thin it with 1 tablespoon vegetable oil or water.

Worcestershire sauce is a thin, pungent dark sauce used to flavor soups, stews, and other sauces. It is a mixture of anchovies, soybeans, tamarind, vinegar, and an assortment of spices that is aged in wooden vats for several years. Store it in a cool, dark spot, where it will stay fresh for many, many months.

CHEESES

Try to keep a good assortment of cheeses on hand. I always make sure to have a chunk of Parmesan cheese for grating over pasta and into sauces, and adding to salads and antipasto platters. The only way to tell if you're buying real Parmigiano-Reggiano in this country, rather than one of the many cheaper, less flavorful imitations, is to look for the words *Parmigiano-Reggiano* imprinted on the rind of every cheese. Unfortunately, real Parmigiano-Reggiano is expensive, but truly worth the price. It is so full of flavor that you need a lot less than you would of an imitation. You can, however, substitute Romano cheese. Pregrated cheeses and imitation Parmesan tend to taste like sawdust. Parmesan should be tightly wrapped and refrigerated. If you buy a large piece, freeze whatever you won't use immediately.

I also like to keep cheddar cheese on hand for melting over sandwiches, pasta dishes, and casseroles; and blue cheese and feta for crumbling into salads and pasta dishes. Cheese should be tightly wrapped and refrigerated.

CHILE PEPPERS

Whenever possible, use fresh chile peppers. I particularly like the jalapeño, a dark, rich green pepper about 2 inches long with a good spicy bite. Serrano peppers are a bit spicier, about 2 to 3 inches long, with a shiny light green color and cylindrical shape. Fresh chile peppers will last for several weeks if they are kept dry and refrigerated.

You can also substitute dried red peppers, available at most grocery stores, for fresh chiles. Dried chiles will keep indefinitely if they are stored in a cool, dark spot.

Serranos and jalapeños also come pickled (in cans), and can be substituted for fresh or dried, if necessary, but they should first be drained, rinsed, and chopped.

Always take care when handling chile peppers—dried or fresh. Don't touch your face or eyes because the oil in the pepper is extremely potent and can burn. Some cooks prefer to wear rubber gloves when handling chiles.

COCONUT

I like to keep a bag of shredded coconut in the freezer. It's ideal to have around for adding to curries, stews, chutneys, or sauces. It also adds good flavor and texture to composed salads.

DRIED FRUITS

Dried figs, apricots, prunes, and dates add a great fruity taste and chewy texture to stuffings, composed salads, stews, and sauces. They should be tightly wrapped and stored in a cool, dark spot.

GARLIC AND GINGER

When I use garlic in a recipe it is always fresh garlic—no powders, pastes, or chopped cloves in oil. Before you chop a clove of garlic, first crush it with the flat side of a large knife or cleaver; the skin will pop off. Garlic should always be sautéed or fried over moderate heat. (The one exception is cooking in a searing hot wok, where the garlic is stir-fried for just a few seconds.) Store garlic in a cool, dark spot, where it will stay fresh for a few weeks. Remove any green center—it is bitter.

Once you've tasted fresh ginger, it's hard to ever use powdered. Fresh ginger has a pungency and flavor that just can't be duplicated by the powdered variety. Using a sharp knife, peel off the thin skin of the gingerroot and then use as directed. Fresh ginger is available in most grocery stores and fruit and vegetable shops, and should be stored, unwrapped, in the refrigerator. It will stay fresh and firm for several weeks; well wrapped it will keep longer in the freezer.

HERBS AND SPICES

I use quite a lot of fresh herbs in my cooking—particularly basil, thyme, rosemary, parsley, chives, and coriander (also called cilantro or Chinese parsley). With leftovers, in particular, herbs can wake up the flavors of the cooked foods. Herbs are easy to grow (whether in a city apartment or a suburban or country garden). Dried herbs can also be used. The general formula for fresh herbs to dried is: 1 tablespoon chopped fresh herb *or* 1 teaspoon crumbled dried herb. Herbs will stay fresh in the refrigerator for several days, wrapped in a slightly damp paper towel or tea towel.

Keep a good assortment of spices on hand as well: ground cinnamon, ground cloves, whole nutmeg (to be freshly grated as needed), curry powder, cumin, turmeric, ground red cayenne, hot and sweet paprika, etc. Never store spices in the sun or near the heat of a stove; the heat will destroy their pungency. Keep in a cool, dark spot.

MUSHROOMS

I try to keep a few varieties of dried mushrooms around—porcini (cêpes), morels, or shiitake. Dried wild mushrooms have a surprising amount of rich, earthy flavor and a wonderful meaty texture. Soak dried mushrooms in a bowl of warm water for about 15 minutes, rinse, drain, and dry before using. Dried mushrooms will keep indefinitely in a tightly sealed jar in a cool, dark spot.

NUTS

Almonds, walnuts, hazelnuts, and pine nuts (also called pignoli) are handy for sprinkling over salads, into sauces, and over meats and fish. Keep nuts fresh in the freezer, and use as needed.

OILS

Olive oil is fruity and delicate, with a subtle olive flavor. To my taste there is no finer oil. An added plus: olive oil is an unsaturated fat; it contains no cholesterol. I generally keep two varieties of olive oil in my pantry—a delicate, light (and expensive) *extra-virgin olive oil* for vinaigrettes, salads, and pasta, and a less costly *virgin* or *pure* or *fine olive oil* for cooking. Store olive oil in a dark bottle (clean wine bottles are ideal), in a cool, dark spot.

Nut oils (walnut, hazelnut, and almond) are particularly rich, and are delicious sprinkled over steamed vegetables, salads, or even pizza. Store them in the refrigerator, as they tend to go rancid quickly.

Safflower, vegetable, and peanut oil are good, light, all-purpose cooking oils. Store in a cool, dark spot, or refrigerate.

Sesame oil, which is used frequently in Oriental dishes and stir-fries, has the rich, intense scent and flavor of toasted sesame seeds. It will stay fresh for several months in a cool, dark spot or refrigerator.

ORIENTAL INGREDIENTS

Chinese chile oil is fiery hot, with the flavor of chile peppers. It's used frequently to season Oriental dishes, marinades, and sauces, and will stay fresh in the refrigerator for several months.

Chinese chile sauce is a thick, spicy paste used to flavor sauces and stir-fries. You can also use *Chinese chile paste* or *black bean paste,* thick chile-and-garlic-filled pastes that should be used in moderation. All of these should be refrigerated after opening.

Chinese fermented black beans are small soybeans that have been fermented and preserved with salt and ginger. Because they are so salty, Chinese black beans should always be rinsed under cold running water, and dried. They are generally chopped and added to stir-fries and sauces. Black beans will keep indefinitely if stored in a cool, dark spot.

Chinese rice vinegar comes in three colors: red, black, and white. *Chinese red vinegar* is made from red rice and is extremely sweet. It's traditionally used to cut the richness of certain foods and to highlight the sweetness of soups, stews, and seafood dishes. *Chinese black vinegar* has a rich, sweet flavor similar to that of a Spanish sherry vinegar or Italian balsamic vinegar. And *Chinese white or pale amber vinegar* is pale-colored and frequently used in sweet-and-sour dishes or as a dressing for salads and raw vegetables. Store in a cool, dark spot.

Chinese rice wine, made from fermented rice, has a clear, slightly golden color and a rich, sweet flavor. It's added to sauces and stir-fries, and used to deglaze pans. Store in a cool, dark spot.

Oyster sauce is a thick, velvety brown sauce made from dried oysters that have been pounded with soy sauce, salt, and other seasonings, and then fermented. It's delicious in sauces, stir-fries, stews, and casseroles. Refrigerated, oyster sauce will stay fresh for several months.

Sake is a sweet-flavored Japanese rice wine. Store in a cool, dark spot.

Sesame oil; see Oils.

Sichuan peppercorns are reddish-brown berries with a strong odor and flavor. Grind and add to soups, stews, sauces, and stir-fries in small quantities. Keep in a tightly sealed jar in a cool, dark spot.

Soy sauce can be used in marinades, sauces, glazes, and dipping sauces. It's also a table condiment that can take the place of salt. The best soy sauce indicates "Naturally Fermented" on the label and is made from only the following ingredients: soybeans, wheat (or flour), salt, and water.

There are several types of soy sauce available today. Chinese soy tends to be stronger and saltier than the Japanese variety, with a more pronounced flavor. Both Chinese and Japanese soy sauces range from Light (also called Pale) to Dark and Heavy. There are now several brands of light soy sauce on the market that are brewed in the traditional manner, but contain up to 43 percent less sodium.

Tamari and soy sauce have an almost identical look, taste, and smell, but tamari contains very little, if any, wheat. (Most soy sauces contain from 30 to 50 percent wheat.) Tamari can be used instead of soy sauce.

All soy sauce and tamari should be stored in the refrigerator or a cool, dark spot.

PASTA AND RICE

I adore pasta and use every size, shape, and color imaginable. Always keep a good assortment on hand—spaghetti, linguine, fettuccine, angel hair, orzo (rice-shaped pasta), Chinese rice noodles, and cellophane noodles.

Rice is one of the most satisfying foods in the world. I always have large jars of brown rice and white rice on hand. I also try to keep a small bag of short-grain Italian rice (Arborio) for making risotto. Store rice in a tightly sealed jar or plastic bag in a cool, dark spot.

SUN-DRIED TOMATOES

Sun-dried tomatoes are exactly what their name describes. Perfectly ripe plum tomatoes are dried under the hot summer sun until they shrivel up and look like dried chile peppers. Like other dried foods, these tomatoes have an intense flavor.

Drying tomatoes in the sun is an Italian tradition. When the drying is complete, the tomatoes take on a rich, dark maroon color and a pleasing, chewy texture.

Sun-dried tomatoes are available in two forms: marinated in olive or vegetable oil and herbs, or dried (reconstitute in warm water for about 10 minutes and then drain before using). Sun-dried tomatoes, particularly those floating in a good-quality olive oil, are not cheap. But their intense flavor goes a long way, and when the tomatoes are gone you're left with a jar of exquisitely seasoned oil—ideal for salads, or for sautéing fish, chicken, or beef. The dried variety will stay fresh in your pantry indefinitely, but the marinated ones should be kept in the refrigerator and used within a couple of months of opening, before the marinating oil goes rancid.

These tomatoes are delicious added to salads, antipasto platters, pizza, sauces, stews, and sandwiches.

TORTILLAS

I always keep a supply of corn and wheat tortillas in the freezer (or the refrigerator for immediate use). They are now available in most grocery stores or specialty food shops and can be bought fresh or frozen. They're easy to heat up (either on a griddle or in a warm oven) and can be filled with leftover meats, poultry, or seafood and topped with a spicy salsa, sour cream or yogurt, guacamole, chopped coriander or parsley, and grated cheese. Tortilla (or taco) chips also come in handy for adding to casseroles or stews, or serving with dips.

VINEGAR

Balsamic vinegar, or *aceto balsamico,* is a richly flavored Italian wine vinegar made by aging fermented wine in wooden casks for anywhere from several months to several years. It has a dark brown color and a sweet, aromatic flavor that is excellent on salads, cold grilled meats, poultry or fish, even sprinkled over fruit and melon.

Cider vinegar, made from fermented apple cider, is excellent in salads, stews, pickles, and chutneys. Look for a brand that indicates that it was "Made from Whole Apples" and "Aged in Wood." The vinegar should also be full strength—5 to 5½ percent acidity.

Wine vinegar is the most versatile type of vinegar. It's worth the few extra dollars to buy a really good, well-aged vinegar—be it red or white. Look for a vinegar that has at least 5% acidity.

All vinegars should be stored in a cool, dark spot or refrigerated.

WINE

Always keep a bottle of good dry red or white table wine around for cooking and deglazing pans. Dry sherry is also handy, and can be used instead of Chinese rice wine in Chinese recipes and marinades. Dry vermouth is useful to have in the refrigerator for adding to marinades, roasting meats and poultry, sautéing fish, and deglazing pans.

1
BEEF

MASTER RECIPES

LEFTOVER RECIPES

MASTER RECIPE:

STANDING RIB ROAST

I don't eat a lot of beef, but when I want to serve something really special I'll go all out and make a standing rib roast. And I always get an extra rib so I know there will be leftovers for days to come. Be sure to throw a few peeled whole onions, a head of garlic (page 49), and medium or baby potatoes in with the roast. Serve with sprigs of fresh watercress.

SERVES 8.

A 5- to 6-pound standing rib roast, about 2 to 3 ribs*
Olive oil
About 6 cloves garlic, peeled and thinly sliced
Freshly ground black pepper
Salt

1. Remove the meat from the refrigerator 2 hours before roasting.
2. Preheat the oven to 500 degrees.
3. Place the meat, fat side up, in a large roasting pan. Very lightly rub the surface and sides of the meat with olive oil.
4. Using a sharp knife, make a few X's in the top of the roast and insert the garlic. Sprinkle the top liberally with the pepper and a touch of salt.
5. Place the roast in the oven and immediately reduce the heat to 350 degrees. Roast the meat for about 1 hour or until the meat reaches an internal temperature of 120 degrees for rare; 135 degrees for medium; and 145 degrees for well-done.
6. Let the meat sit for about 15 to 20 minutes before serving.

*Ask the butcher to remove the chine, or backbone, and tie it back on to give the meat a natural rack to roast on.

MASTER RECIPE:

BOILED BEEF (POT-AU-FEU)

In New England it's called a boiled beef supper; Italians refer to it as *bollito misto;* the French name for it is pot-au-feu. Whatever you call it, beef simmered in a homemade beef stock, accompanied by an assortment of vegetables and potatoes, can be a culinary masterpiece—simple, hearty, and satisfying.

The key to a good boiled beef is a cut of beef—happily, in this case, an inexpensive cut—that will stand up to several hours of cooking. And, despite the name, the beef should never actually boil; you want it to *gently* simmer for several hours. And, if at all possible, use a homemade beef stock (page 18) and a variety of very fresh vegetables. The list of vegetables is meant only as a suggestion; use all or some of them, add a cored, quartered cabbage or any other vegetable that will hold up to 20 minutes of simmering.

You can serve this dish in two courses—first the rich beef broth, sprinkled with fresh minced parsley, followed by the sliced meat and vegetables—or simply serve the thinly sliced meat, surrounded by the cooked vegetables, with a few spoonfuls of hot broth poured over it all. Serve some of the hot broth in a gravy boat. (You can strain and freeze the remaining broth for a future soup, stew, or sauce.)

Serve the boiled beef with grated horseradish, an assortment of mustards, or a green sauce (page 235).

SERVES 8.

About 10 cups homemade beef stock (page 18), or canned stock
1 bay leaf
2 cloves garlic, peeled
About 5 pounds boneless beef (brisket, rump, boneless chuck, short
    ribs, or bottom round), tied
About 6 medium potatoes, peeled and quartered, or 3 cups cooked
    potatoes, quartered
2 cups small white onions, peeled
2 cups julienne strips carrots
2 cups julienne strips parsnips and/or turnips
2 cups julienne strips leeks
1/4 cup minced fresh parsley

1. In a large stockpot, bring the stock, bay leaf, and garlic to a boil over high heat. Remove any foam that rises to the surface. Add the meat, cover, and reduce the heat to low, in order to create a very gentle simmer. The stock should completely cover the beef; if it does not, simply add more stock or water. Simmer until the meat is just tender when pierced with a fork, about 2 to 3 hours, depending on the cut of meat, skimming off any foam that rises to the surface during the cooking.

2. If using raw potatoes, bring a large pot of water to a boil. Add the potatoes, cover, and boil until almost tender, about 8 to 10 minutes. Drain and reserve. (The recipe can be made ahead up to this point.)

3. When the meat is nearly tender, add the onions, carrots, parsnips and/or turnips, and leeks. Let simmer about 20 to 25 minutes, or until tender. During the last 5 minutes of cooking, add the cooked potatoes.

4. Remove the meat and let it sit for about 10 minutes before carving. Take off the string and slice the meat. Serve on a large platter, surrounded by the cooked vegetables and potatoes. Sprinkle with the parsley.

MASTER RECIPE:

GRILLED STEAK WITH PROVENÇAL HERBS

SERVES 4.

**Four 1½-inch-thick 12-ounce steaks (New York, Delmonico, or other
  cut)**
1 tablespoon olive oil
2 garlic cloves, minced
2 teaspoons minced fresh rosemary, or 1 teaspoon crumbled dried
2 teaspoons minced fresh thyme, or 1 teaspoon crumbled dried
2 teaspoons chopped fresh basil, or 1 teaspoon crumbled dried
Freshly ground black pepper

1. Place the steaks in a shallow dish. Rub both sides with the oil, garlic, and herbs. Season with the pepper. Let stand 1 hour before cooking.

2. Preheat the broiler or barbecue. Cook the steaks 2 inches from the heat source to desired doneness, about 4 minutes per side for rare.

MASTER RECIPE:

BRISKET SMOTHERED IN ONIONS

Susan Friedland, my editor, told me about this recipe, and to be perfectly honest, I didn't quite believe in it until I gave it a try. A brisket of beef is covered with *lots* of onions, a touch of salt and pepper, and baked in a low oven. The result: an exceptionally succulent piece of meat with a rich, oniony sauce. The onions and natural gravy can be served as is or pureed in a blender or food processor.

Serve with horseradish and/or applesauce.

SERVES 6 TO 8.

A 6-pound brisket of beef
Salt
Freshly ground black pepper
3 pounds onions, sliced

1. Preheat the oven to 300 degrees.
2. Lightly season the brisket and place in a casserole. Sprinkle the onions over the meat. Cover the casserole and bake for about 2½ hours, or until the meat is very tender.
3. Slice the meat on the diagonal and serve with the onions and gravy on top.

CORNED BEEF AND CABBAGE

It always takes St. Patrick's Day to motivate me to make this deeply satisfying dish. Nothing could be easier: a pickled brisket of beef and a few seasonings are slowly simmered in a pot of water for several hours. The cabbage can either be steamed separately or added to the simmering beef during the last few minutes of cooking. The key to really good corned beef is *slow* simmering.

Serve with boiled potatoes, a variety of mustards, and a pot of strong horseradish.

SERVES 4.

A 4 1/2-pound corned beef
1 bay leaf
1 onion, halved
8 peppercorns
1 large white cabbage, quartered and cored

1. Place the beef, bay leaf, onion, and peppercorns in a large pot and cover with cold water. Bring to a boil over high heat, reduce the heat to low, cover partially, and simmer for about 4 hours, or about 1 hour per pound. To test for doneness, stick a fork into the center of the meat; it should feel very tender.

2. Bring a pot of water, plus 1 cup of the beef broth, to a boil. Place the cabbage quarters in a vegetable steamer and steam over the boiling water/broth until tender, about 10 to 15 minutes. Remove from the steamer and place on a serving plate. Add 2 tablespoons broth from the beef pot and salt and pepper to taste. Or, during the last 10 minutes of cooking, add the cabbage to the simmering meat and cook until just tender.

3. Using a large slotted spoon, remove the meat and cabbage and place on a serving platter. Thinly slice the meat on the diagonal.

MASTER RECIPE:

MEAT STOCK

Unlike the other stock recipes given in this book, this one uses fresh (not cooked and leftover) meat to create a very rich and flavorful stock. Use it as a base for sauces and soups.

MAKES ABOUT 6 CUPS.

About 2 to 3 pounds of bones—beef, veal, or lamb
1 large onion, quartered
2 carrots, cut into chunks
2 stalks celery, cut into chunks
1 cup dry white or red wine
1 bay leaf
6 peppercorns
Salt
Freshly ground black pepper

1. Preheat the oven to 400 degrees.
2. Place the bones in a roasting pan along with the onion, carrots, and celery. Roast for about 20 minutes, or until beginning to brown. Remove from the oven and deglaze the pan with the wine.
3. Pour the bones, vegetables, wine, and any bits and pieces clinging to the pan into a large stockpot. Add the bay leaf and peppercorns and cover completely with water. Bring to a boil over high heat, reduce, and let the stock simmer, partially covered, for about an hour. Season to taste with salt and pepper. If the stock still tastes weak, simmer another 15 to 30 minutes, uncovered.
4. Skim off any fat that is floating on the top. Use, or refrigerate and freeze the stock until needed.

BEEF SANDWICH IDEAS

➤Roast beef with garlic herb cheese, thinly sliced red onions, and to-matoes on black bread.

➤Cold beef with green peppercorn mustard and thin slices of onion on French bread.

➤Thinly sliced beef on a hard roll smothered with sautéed red and green onions and melted cheese.

➤Warm beef slices on a toasted baguette or hard roll with garlic-flavored mayonnaise.

➤Cold steak sandwich on French bread with watercress butter (blend 1 stick soft butter and 1/2 cup very finely chopped or pureed water-cress).

➤Paper-thin slices of cold roast beef layered with arugula, sun-dried tomatoes, and mozzarella cheese, drizzled with olive oil and red wine vinegar on a loaf of Italian peasant bread.

➤Cold beef sandwich with cucumbers and a curry-cumin mayonnaise (mix 1/2 cup mayonnaise with 1 teaspoon ground curry powder and 1/2 teaspoon ground cumin).

➤Thinly sliced beef in a warm corn tortilla topped with guacamole, salsa, shredded lettuce, and chopped fresh coriander.

➤Thinly sliced beef and Brie on crusty bread, placed under the broiler until the cheese is melted and bubbling, and topped with chopped walnuts or almonds.

Open-Faced Roast Beef Sandwich
with a Shallot-Mustard-Cream Sauce

This is a variation on the standard open-faced roast beef sandwich you find in many restaurants. There is quite a bit of sauce for each sandwich, but if you're like me, you'll want a little extra to sop up with the French bread. The amounts given below are enough for two sandwiches, but the recipe can easily be doubled or tripled.

SERVES 2.

4 teaspoons butter
2 teaspoons olive oil
Tiny bit of roast beef fat, minced (optional)
4 tablespoons minced shallots or onion
1 cup beef stock (page 18)
1 tablespoon grainy mustard*
1/3 cup heavy cream
Very generous grinding of black pepper
2 teaspoons natural juices or gravy from the roast beef (optional)
A 10-inch loaf of crusty French bread
About 6 slices cooked roast beef, with fat removed
1 tablespoon minced fresh parsley
1 tablespoon minced fresh chervil or chives

1. In a small saucepan, heat 2 teaspoons of the butter, the olive oil, and optional roast beef fat. Add the shallots and sauté over moderately low heat for about 5 minutes, or until softened but not brown. Add the broth and bring to a boil over high heat. Reduce the heat to moderate and add the mustard, cream, pepper, and roast beef juices. Let simmer for about 5 to 10 minutes, or until reduced and thick enough to heavily coat the back of a spoon.

2. Meanwhile, slice the French bread in half and then in half again lengthwise. Toast in a 250 degree oven for about 5 minutes, or until warm and very lightly browned.

3. In a medium skillet, heat the remaining 2 teaspoons of butter over moderate heat. Add the roast beef and sauté about 30 seconds on each side, until warm and just beginning to brown.

4. Place the bread on a serving plate, top with the beef, and spoon the sauce on top. Sprinkle with the chopped herbs and serve warm.

*Grainy mustard gives this sauce a wonderful crunchy texture. If it is unavailable, use a sharp, smooth Dijon mustard.

■■
Mexican Steak Sandwich with Avocado Cream

Thin slices of steak are placed in a warm tortilla, then spread with a spicy, creamy avocado mixture and topped with fresh salsa. Although this recipe involves several steps, don't be scared away. The salsa can be made in minutes; preparing the avocado sauce is simply a matter of combining avocado and sour cream; and the steak is reheated just briefly. For variety, spread a layer of warm refried beans on top of the avocado cream.

This recipe makes enough for two sandwiches; it can easily be doubled or tripled, depending on the amount of leftover steak you have.

SERVES 2.

The Salsa:
2 small ripe tomatoes, or 1 medium, chopped into small cubes
$^1/_3$ cup finely chopped red onion
1 scallion, thinly sliced
1 garlic clove, minced
1 tablespoon finely chopped jalapeño pepper, or about 1 teaspoon
   Tabasco or other liquid hot pepper sauce to taste
Juice of 1 lime
1 tablespoon olive oil

The Avocado Cream:
$^1/_2$ ripe avocado, peeled
2 tablespoons sour cream or yogurt
1 tablespoon finely chopped jalapeño pepper, or to taste, or 1
   teaspoon Tabasco or other liquid hot pepper sauce to taste

The Sandwich:
2 large wheat or corn tortillas
$^1/_2$ tablespoon butter
8 $^1/_4$-inch-thick slices cooked steak or roast beef, well trimmed
$^1/_2$ ripe avocado, peeled and cut into thin slices
1 tablespoon sour cream or yogurt

1. Prepare the salsa: Mix the tomatoes, onion, scallion, garlic, and pepper or hot pepper sauce. Stir in the lime juice and oil. Cover and refrigerate for at least 1 hour.

2. Make the avocado cream: In a small bowl, mash the avocado with

the back of a fork. Mix in the sour cream or yogurt; add the pepper or hot pepper sauce. (The avocado cream should be fairly spicy.)

3. Make the sandwich: In a very low oven, heat the tortillas until warm but not hot or brittle, about 1 minute on each side. In a medium skillet, melt the butter over medium heat. Add the steak and sauté about 30 seconds on each side, or until warm.

4. Dividing the mixture equally, spread the warm tortillas with the avocado cream. Spread the meat on top and surround with the avocado slices. Top with about 2 tablespoons of the salsa and ½ tablespoon of sour cream or yogurt. To eat, roll the tortilla up. Serve the remaining salsa on the side.

■■

Brisket Sandwich with Apple and Red Horseradish Mayonnaise

Serve with ice-cold mugs of dark beer and homemade potato chips (page 133).

SERVES 2.

4 to 5 tablespoons mayonnaise
2 to 3 tablespoons drained horseradish with beets (red horseradish)
4 thin slices rye bread with caraway seeds
6 to 8 thin slices cooked brisket, steak, or roast beef
1 Granny Smith or other tart apple, cored and very thinly sliced
Several sprigs of fresh dill
Generous grinding of black pepper
Several leaves red leaf or iceberg lettuce or watercress, chopped into
    bite-sized pieces

1. Mix the mayonnaise and horseradish and spread generously on each slice of rye bread. Top two of the slices with the brisket, slightly overlapping each piece of meat. Place the apple slices, dill, and pepper on top. Put the lettuce or watercress on top of that and close the sandwiches with the other two slices of bread.

2. Serve with additional apple slices and a dill sprig on each plate.

■■

Reuben Sandwich

This is a bizarre, though classic, combination: corned beef, Russian dressing, cheese, and sauerkraut sandwiched between two slices of rye bread. What makes this version so delicious is that the Russian dressing is spiked with horseradish and tart capers and the sandwich is first baked and then sautéed with butter to give it a golden-brown finish.

SERVES 2.

Russian Dressing:
    4 tablespoons mayonnaise, preferably homemade
    2 tablespoons ketchup
    2 tablespoons drained capers or chopped gherkin pickles
    2 teaspoons drained prepared horseradish

The Sandwich:
    4 slices rye bread
    6 thin slices of cheddar, Swiss, or other hard cheese
    6 to 8 thin slices cooked corned beef or boiled beef
    $1/2$ cup drained sauerkraut
    3 tablespoons butter

1. Prepare the Russian dressing: In a small bowl, mix all the ingredients. Taste for seasoning and add more horseradish if you want a spicier dressing.
2. Preheat the oven to 400 degrees.
3. Assemble the sandwich: Spread a thin layer of the Russian dressing on each of the four slices of bread. Place the cheese on two slices of bread. Top with the corned beef and sauerkraut and close the sandwiches with the other two slices of bread. Wrap tightly in aluminum foil and bake for 15 minutes.
4. Place half the butter in a skillet large enough to hold both sandwiches and melt over moderately high heat. Remove the sandwiches from the oven and the foil and place in the skillet. Sauté for about 2 minutes on one side, and remove to a plate. Add the remaining butter to the skillet, flip sandwich to the other side and sauté another 2 minutes. Serve hot, straight from the skillet.

Steak and Potato Salad
with Horseradish Vinaigrette

SERVES 2 TO 3.

The Vinaigrette:
- 3 teaspoons Dijon mustard
- 2 tablespoons freshly grated horseradish, or 1 tablespoon drained prepared white horseradish*
- 4 tablespoons olive oil
- 2 tablespoons white or red wine vinegar
- Salt
- Freshly ground black pepper
- 3 scallions, thinly sliced

The Salad:
- 1½ cups assorted greens (arugula, buttercrunch lettuce, watercress)
- 4 small red potatoes, or 2 large baking potatoes, cooked, peeled, and cut into small wedges
- About 8 thin slices cooked steak or roast beef

1. Prepare the vinaigrette: In a small bowl, mix together the mustard and horseradish. Whisk in the oil and vinegar. Add the salt, pepper, and half the scallions; taste for seasoning. The vinaigrette should have a sharp bite. Season to taste with additional mustard, horseradish, or salt and pepper, as needed.

2. Assemble the salad: Place the assorted greens on a large serving plate. Arrange the potatoes and steak in the center of the greens and drizzle the vinaigrette over the entire salad. Sprinkle the remaining scallions on top.

*Try to find fresh horseradish root for this recipe. Peel the root and grate it over a small bowl.

Spring Steak and Asparagus Salad

This is an extremely colorful salad that celebrates the fresh flavors of spring. Cold slices of steak and cooked asparagus are topped with a red pepper and cornichon vinaigrette and then garnished with red pepper strips and crumbled feta cheese. The salad is delicious served with warm pita, French bread, or buttered toast.

This salad can be put together in just a few minutes if the asparagus is cooked ahead. To prepare the asparagus, trim their light-colored or white ends and place in a skillet of cold water. Simmer for 6 to 8 minutes, depending on the thickness, or until just tender. Drain and place in a skillet of cold water to prevent further cooking. Drain again and set aside.

SERVES 2 TO 4.

The Vinaigrette:
2 tablespoons thinly sliced cornichons or gherkins
$2^1/_2$ tablespoons seeded and finely chopped red bell pepper
1 scallion, thinly sliced
$1^1/_2$ tablespoons red wine vinegar
3 tablespoons olive oil
Salt
Freshly ground black pepper

The Salad:
$^1/_2$ pound cooked asparagus (see headnote)
About 10 thin slices cooked steak or roast beef (about 2 cups)
4 thin slices red bell pepper
$^1/_2$ cup finely crumbled feta or Roquefort cheese

1. Prepare the vinaigrette: In a small bowl, combine the cornichons, red pepper, and scallion. Mix in the vinegar and oil and add salt and pepper to taste. Set aside.

2. Assemble the salad: Put the cooked asparagus in the center of a large serving plate. Place the steak slices on either side, fanning them out slightly. Spoon the vinaigrette evenly over the meat and asparagus. Lay the red pepper slices on the asparagus and crumble the cheese over the meat slices. (The salad can be served immediately or allowed to marinate for up to 2 hours at room temperature.)

██

Thai Beef Salad

Thai salads traditionally include *nam pla*, a dark, salty sauce made of fermented fish. To a western palate, the fishy flavor may not be pleasing, so I use soy sauce instead. Fresh mint and coriander are essential to the success of this salad, full of intriguing and exotic flavors.

SERVES 2.

The Sweet and Spicy Sauce:

4 garlic cloves, chopped

2 very small dried red chile peppers, with the seeds removed from one*

1½ teaspoons sugar

Juice of 2 limes or 1 large lemon

1 tablespoon soy sauce or fish sauce

1 tablespoon orange juice

1 teaspoon chopped fresh coriander

1 teaspoon chopped fresh mint

The Salad:

4 lettuce leaves, thinly sliced (iceberg, romaine, or red leaf)

1 tablespoon coarsely chopped fresh mint leaves

1 tablespoon coarsely chopped fresh coriander leaves

About 10 ¼-inch-thick slices cooked steak or roast beef, preferably rare

1 cup peeled and thinly sliced cucumber

3 scallions, sliced lengthwise and cut into 2-inch pieces

1 large onion, thinly sliced and quartered

1. Make the sauce: Place the garlic and chile peppers in a mortar and crush with a pestle to form a paste. (If you don't have a mortar and pestle, simply use the back of a wooden spoon and crush the ingredients in a small bowl.) Add the sugar and crush until a thick paste is formed. Put the paste in a small bowl and mix in the lime juice, soy sauce, orange juice, coriander, and mint. Set aside. (The sauce can be made several hours ahead.)

2. Assemble the salad: Mix the lettuce, mint, and coriander and place in the center of a serving plate. Layer the beef on top of the greens and surround with the cucumber, scallion, and orange segments. Drizzle the sauce over the salad and serve at room temperature.

*If you want a very spicy sauce include the seeds from both chiles.

Celery Remoulade with Julienne
of Roast Beef and Red Pepper

Your mouth is treated to a wonderful combination of textures and flavors in this dish. Plan to make it 2 or 3 hours before serving so the flavors come together.

SERVES 2 TO 4.

> **2 cups julienne strips celery root (celeriac)**
> **1 teaspoon salt**
> **3 tablespoons fresh lemon juice**
> **1 tablespoon drained prepared horseradish**
> **1 1/2 tablespoons Dijon mustard**
> **Salt**
> **Freshly ground black pepper**
> **1/4 cup mayonnaise, preferably homemade**
> **1 cup julienne strips roast or boiled beef**
> **1/2 cup julienne strips red bell pepper**

1. In a small bowl, toss the celery root with the salt and 1 teaspoon lemon juice and let sit for 30 minutes. Rinse off the salt and lemon, drain, and dry. (This process softens the celery root.)
2. In a medium serving bowl, mix the remaining lemon juice with the horseradish, mustard, salt, and pepper. Stir in the mayonnaise to create a smooth sauce. Gently fold in the celery root, beef, and red pepper. Taste for seasoning. Marinate for 2 to 3 hours before serving.

Medallion of Beef Salad
with Horseradish Sauce

SERVES 2 TO 4.

> **1 cup heavy cream**
> **3 tablespoons drained prepared horseradish**
> **2 teaspoons fresh lemon juice**

About ¼ teaspoon Tabasco or other liquid hot pepper sauce
3 cups mixed salad greens
About 10 thin slices cooked roast beef or steak
1 cup sliced scallions and/or red pepper strips

1. Whip the cream until it forms peaks. Gently fold in the horseradish, lemon juice, and Tabasco. Taste for seasoning and add more Tabasco if desired. The sauce can be refrigerated for 2 to 3 hours before serving.

2. Place the greens on a large platter, top with the beef, and scatter the scallions and/or red pepper strips around the meat.

3. Spoon the sauce over the beef or serve it on the side.

■■

Corned Beef and Oriental Cabbage Salad

The pickled flavor of the corned beef is delicious with this ginger-sesame-and-soy-flavored cabbage salad.

SERVES 2.

1 cup very thinly sliced cabbage
1½ tablespoons soy sauce
1 tablespoon Chinese rice wine or dry sherry
1 tablespoon wine vinegar or cider vinegar
1½ teaspoons sesame oil
1 teaspoon minced fresh ginger
1 teaspoon sugar
4 to 6 thin slices cooked corned beef or boiled beef

1. In a bowl, mix the cabbage with all the ingredients except the corned beef, and marinate 1 hour.

2. Remove the cabbage from the bowl using a slotted spoon and place in the center of a serving plate. Cut the beef on the diagonal into 3-inch-long strips. Place the beef over the cabbage in a line and drizzle with the remaining marinade.

Stir-Fried Steak with Broccoli, Cashews, and Spicy Nut Sauce

Serve with steamed rice, scallions, and additional hot sauce on the side.

SERVES 2.

The Spicy Nut Sauce:

2 tablespoons peanut butter

4 tablespoons Chinese rice wine or dry sherry

2 tablespoons soy sauce

1 tablespoon sesame oil

1 tablespoon honey or sugar

About 1 teaspoon hot Chinese chile paste or Tabasco

The Steak and Vegetables:

2 tablespoons vegetable or peanut oil

3 garlic cloves, minced

1 1/2 cups broccoli florets

1/4 cup cashew nuts

2 scallions, thinly sliced

8 1/4-inch-thick slices steak

2 scallions, halved lengthwise and cut into 2-inch pieces

1. Make the sauce: Place peanut butter in a small bowl. Add the rice wine, 3 tablespoons water, and soy sauce, stirring until smooth. Add the remaining sauce ingredients. Taste for seasoning, adding more chile paste if you want the dish to be very spicy. Set aside.

2. Prepare the steak and vegetables: Heat a wok or large skillet over high heat. Add 1 tablespoon of the oil and let it get hot. Add the garlic and broccoli and stir-fry for about a minute. Add about 1 1/2 tablespoons water to help the broccoli cook and keep it from burning. Stir until the broccoli is just cooked, but still crispy. Remove broccoli and garlic to a plate.

3. Add the remaining tablespoon of oil to the wok. When hot, add the nuts and stir for about 30 seconds. Add the thinly sliced scallions and beef and stir another 30 seconds. Add broccoli and the spicy nut sauce and stir for about 15 seconds. Serve garnished with sliced scallions.

Japanese-Style Beef Rolls with Scallions

This dish will only work with roast beef that is rare to medium-rare. Serve these rolls as a first course or hors d'oeuvre.

MAKES 12 BITE-SIZED PIECES.

18 scallions
1 tablespoon vegetable oil
3 garlic cloves, thinly sliced
3 tablespoons soy sauce
4 tablespoons sake, Chinese rice wine, or dry sherry
1 1/2 tablespoons sesame oil
6 *very thinly* sliced pieces of cooked rare steak or roast beef

1. Cut the scallions into 2-inch-long pieces.
2. Heat the oil in a medium skillet over moderately low heat. Add the scallions and garlic and sauté for about 2 minutes. Add half the soy sauce, half the sake, and 1 tablespoon of the sesame oil, cover the skillet, and braise the scallions and garlic for 3 to 4 minutes, or until softened.
3. Transfer the scallion mixture to a plate and divide it into sixths. Place one-sixth of the mixture in the center of a piece of meat and roll tightly, securing with a toothpick or small piece of string. Place the beef rolls in an ovenproof skillet and sprinkle with the remaining soy, sake, and sesame oil. (Can be made several hours ahead up to this point.)
4. Preheat the broiler and broil for 2 1/2 to 3 minutes, or until the beef is hot and the sauce is bubbling. Place the beef on a serving plate, remove the toothpick or string, cut each roll in half crosswise, and drizzle the sauce from the skillet on top.

Beef with Wasabi and Croutons

This hors d'oeuvre was inspired by Philip McGuire, chef of the Blue Strawberry restaurant in Portsmouth, New Hampshire. Wasabi, the Japanese word for mountain hollyhock, is a fiery hot green horseradish root that grows wild throughout Japan. Fresh wasabi root is difficult to find, but dry powdered wasabi is available in Oriental and specialty food shops. This spicy paste is spread on croutons and topped with thin slices of cooked beef. (Beware the wasabi; the first time I tasted this dish I thought the wasabi was a green herb butter and spread it on the toast lavishly!) McGuire's version was made with smoked medallions of beef, but plain cooked steak or roast beef works equally well.

SERVES ABOUT 6.

1 loaf French bread
2¹/₂ tablespoons wasabi powder
2 to 3 cups thin, 2-inch-long slices cooked steak or roast beef

1. Thinly slice the bread and toast on both sides in a 350 degree oven until lightly browned. Place on a serving plate and set aside.
2. Mix the wasabi powder with enough cold water to make a thick paste. Place in a small serving bowl.
3. Serve the beef with the toast and wasabi at room temperature. Assemble the "sandwich" by spreading a tiny bit of wasabi on each piece of toast and then topping with a strip of beef.

Ma Po Dofu
(Spicy Sichuan-Style Tofu)

This is a homey, one-dish dinner of tofu stir-fried with bits of chopped beef, scallions, and ginger in a very spicy, chile-flavored broth. I've served this stew to people who claim they hate tofu, and they loved it. Serve over steamed white or brown rice.

SERVES 2 TO 3.

    1 tablespoon vegetable or peanut oil
    6 scallions, thinly sliced
    1½ tablespoons minced fresh ginger
    3 garlic cloves, minced
    ½ to 1 tablespoon Chinese chile paste
    ½ to 1 tablespoon Chinese black bean paste
    2 tablespoons Chinese fermented black beans, rinsed and chopped
    1½ tablespoons light soy sauce
    ½ teaspoon crushed Sichuan peppercorns (optional)
    1½ cups chicken stock, preferably homemade (page 193)
    1 pound fresh tofu (bean curd), sliced into 1½-inch cubes
    ½ to ¾ cup very finely chopped cooked steak or beef, or crumbled cooked hamburger, or ½ to ¾ cup finely chopped cooked pork
    1 tablespoon cornstarch
    4 tablespoons chopped fresh cilantro

1. In a wok or a large skillet, heat the oil over high heat. Add half each of the scallions, ginger, and garlic and cook about 30 seconds. Stir in the chile paste, black bean paste, black beans, soy sauce, and peppercorns. Add the chicken stock and bring the mixture to a boil.

2. Gently slide in the tofu, chopped meat, and the remaining ginger and garlic. Simmer for about 3 minutes.

3. In a small bowl, make a thin paste with the cornstarch and about 2 tablespoons of the hot chicken broth from the wok. Slowly add the paste to the wok and simmer for about 1 minute, until slightly thickened. Stir in 1 tablespoon of the cilantro and taste for seasoning. The stew should be spicy, but remember that the rice will offset the spiciness. Add a touch more chile paste if you want a spicier dish.

4. Serve over bowls of white or brown rice and pass the remaining sliced scallions and chopped cilantro in small bowls separately.

Steak in Red-Wine-Mushroom-Cream Sauce

Reminiscent of beef Stroganoff, but lighter and fresher-tasting, this should be served with white rice or noodles.

SERVES 2.

1 tablespoon butter
1 teaspoon vegetable oil
1/3 cup finely chopped onion
1 cup sliced mushrooms
1 teaspoon crumbled dried thyme, or 2 teaspoons minced fresh
1/2 cup red wine
1/3 cup heavy cream
1 teaspoon Dijon mustard
10 1/4-inch-thick slices cooked steak or roast beef
Generous grinding of fresh black pepper
2 tablespoons finely chopped fresh parsley

1. In a medium saucepan, heat half the butter and the oil over moderate heat. Add the onion and sauté until soft but not brown, 3 to 4 minutes. Add the mushrooms and the thyme and stir. Raise the heat to high and add the red wine. Bring to a boil, reduce the heat, and let simmer about 2 minutes. Add the cream and simmer about 3 to 5 minutes, or until slightly thickened. Stir in the mustard.

2. Meanwhile, in a large skillet heat the remaining butter over moderate heat. Sauté the steak slices about 30 seconds to 1 minute on each side, or until warmed through. Sprinkle generously with the pepper and place the hot steak on a serving platter.

3. Spoon the sauce over the steak and sprinkle with the parsley.

Roast Beef Hash

Fresh herbs really wake up the flavor of this classic dish. I've used sage and thyme here, but feel free to experiment with your favorites. Serve accompanied by a jar of hot pepper sauce on the side.

You can make this hash with roast beef, corned beef, boiled beef, brisket, or just about any other cut. It's also delicious made with chicken or turkey.

SERVES 2 TO 3.

2½ tablespoons beef drippings, or vegetable or safflower oil
1 medium onion, minced
1 cup peeled and cubed cooked potatoes
2 cups cubed or thinly shredded cooked roast beef
1 tablespoon chopped fresh sage, or 1 teaspoon crumbled dried
½ tablespoon chopped fresh thyme, or ½ teaspoon crumbled dried
Tabasco or other liquid hot pepper sauce
Salt
Freshly ground black pepper
½ cup heavy cream
3 eggs, poached
3 slices toast

1. In a medium heavy skillet, heat the beef drippings or oil over moderate heat. Sauté the onion until soft and golden, about 5 minutes. Gently stir in the potatoes and cook about 2 minutes. Reduce the heat to low, and very gently stir in the beef, herbs, a generous splash of Tabasco, salt, and pepper. Press the mixture down into a large pancake. Add the cream and press down again, letting the cream seep into the hash mixture. Cook for about 20 to 30 minutes, or until the hash has a golden crust on the bottom. (To check, use a spatula and gently peek under the mixture.)

2. Serve in wedges with poached eggs and toast.

Corned Beef and Cabbage Hash

This recipe is a twist on the traditional combination of corned beef and cabbage. The cabbage adds a subtle sweetness and fresh, slightly crunchy texture to the hash.

SERVES 2.

$^1/_2$ tablespoon butter
$^1/_2$ tablespoon safflower or vegetable oil
$^1/_4$ cup chopped onion
$^1/_2$ cup shredded or very thinly sliced red or white cabbage
$^1/_2$ cup peeled and cubed cooked potatoes
$1^1/_2$ cups cubed or thinly shredded cooked corned beef
Freshly ground black pepper
2 eggs, poached
2 slices toast

1. In a skillet, heat the butter and oil over moderate heat. Sauté the onion for about 5 minutes, or until soft and golden brown. (Do not let it burn.)
2. Add the cabbage and sauté for 3 minutes, until just soft. Add the potatoes, corned beef, and a generous sprinkling of pepper. (You won't need salt because of the saltiness of the meat.) Cook for about 5 minutes. Serve topped with poached eggs and accompany with the toast.

Red Flannel Hash

Diced cooked beets turn a regular beef hash into a slightly sweet traditional New England favorite—Red Flannel Hash.

SERVES 2.

Follow the recipe above for Roast Beef Hash or Corned Beef and Cabbage Hash, and add $^3/_4$ cup diced cooked beet along with the potatoes. You can also substitute $^1/_2$ cup leeks, sautéed until soft but not brown, for the cabbage.

■■■

Corned Beef Carbonara

The classic Italian dish *spaghetti carbonara* combines pasta with a sauce made from raw eggs, bits of *pancetta* ham or smoky bacon, grated Parmesan cheese, and fresh parsley. In this adaptation I substituted corned beef for the ham and found that the meat's subtle saltiness works equally well.

SERVES 2.

1 tablespoon olive oil
1 small onion, thinly sliced
1 small garlic clove, chopped
1 egg
1/2 cup plus 2 tablespoons freshly grated Parmesan cheese, or 1/4 cup
    grated Parmesan and 1/4 cup grated Romano cheese, plus 1
    tablespoon each Parmesan and Romano
3 tablespoons chopped fresh parsley
Salt
Freshly ground black pepper
1/2 pound spaghetti or linguine
1/2 cup julienne strips cooked corned beef
1/8 cup dry white wine
Additional grated Parmesan or Romano cheese

1. In a medium skillet heat the oil over moderate heat. Sauté the onion and garlic for about 5 minutes, or until soft and lightly golden.

2. Meanwhile, bring to a boil a large pot of lightly salted water for the pasta.

3. In a serving bowl, whisk the egg vigorously. Stir in the cheese, half the parsley, and season with salt and a generous grinding of pepper.

4. Boil the pasta until cooked *al dente,* about 8 to 12 minutes, depending on the size. (Fresh pasta only needs to cook about 1 1/2 minutes.)

5. Add the corned beef to the skillet with the onion and raise the heat to high. Add the wine, bring to a boil, then turn off the heat.

6. Drain the cooked pasta and stir immediately with the raw egg mixture in the serving bowl. Top with the corned beef and onion mixture and toss well. Sprinkle with remaining parsley on top and serve additional grated cheese on the side.

Henry VIII Broiled Beef Bones
with Yorkshire-Style Pudding

The gluttonous Henry VIII would have enjoyed gnawing on these delicately flavored bones. Leftover batter can be used to make a delicious pudding that is reminiscent of Yorkshire pudding. The pudding takes the same amount of cooking time as the beef bones.

SERVES 1 TO 2.

1 egg
$^1/_2$ cup milk
1 teaspoon Worcestershire sauce
Splash of Tabasco or other liquid hot pepper sauce
$^1/_2$ cup flour
$^1/_4$ cup bread crumbs (page 46)
Salt
Freshly ground black pepper
2 bones from a cooked standing rib roast, with plenty of meat still
    clinging to them, and excess fat trimmed off
Beef drippings or oil for pudding

1. Preheat the oven to 400 degrees.
2. In a bowl, vigorously whisk the egg, milk, Worcestershire sauce, and Tabasco. On a plate, mix the flour, bread crumbs, salt, and pepper. Dip the bones in the egg mixture, coating them completely. Dip in the flour/bread crumb mixture and shake off any excess coating.
3. Place the bones in an ovenproof skillet. Bake for 20 minutes and then broil for about 2 minutes, or until golden brown.
4. To make the pudding, combine the remaining egg mixture with the flour/bread crumbs. Whisk vigorously for about 5 minutes, until light and fluffy. Melt a bit of beef drippings or oil in the bottom of a small (6- to 8-inch), shallow ovenproof casserole or skillet and add the pudding mixture. Bake for about 20 minutes, or until puffed and golden brown.

SEE ALSO:

2

BREAD

MASTER RECIPE

LEFTOVER RECIPES

MASTER RECIPE:

DOUBLE CHOCOLATE BREAD

Johanne Killeen and her husband, George Germon, run two of the most exciting restaurants in the country, Al Forno and Lucky's, both at 577 South Main Street in downtown Providence, Rhode Island. If you can find any excuse to be in Providence, make sure you get to one of these restaurants. You won't be disappointed.

This recipe, from Killeen and Germon, is a rich, moist double chocolate bread—a cross between a brownie and a slice of chocolate fudge bread. Serve it thinly sliced for teatime or dessert, topped with whipped cream, ice cream, or even hot fudge. If you have a weakness for chocolate, be sure to bake two loaves at a time. You will definitely want to have enough left over to make the exquisite chocolate bread pudding that follows.

SERVES 6 TO 8.

> 1 1/2 cups flour
> 3/4 cup Dutch process cocoa
> 2 teaspoons double-acting baking powder
> 1/2 teaspoon baking soda
> 1/4 teaspoon salt
> 1 stick butter, softened
> 1 cup sugar
> 2 eggs
> 1/2 cup sour cream
> 4 ounces unsweetened chocolate, chopped

1. Preheat the oven to 350 degrees. Lightly butter and flour a 9 × 5 × 3-inch loaf pan and set aside.

2. Sift together the flour, cocoa, baking powder, baking soda, and salt; set aside.

3. Beat the butter and sugar together until light and fluffy. Add the eggs, one at a time, beating about 1 minute after each addition. Add the sifted ingredients alternately with the sour cream and chocolate chunks, beginning and ending with the dry ingredients. (The batter will be quite thick at this point.) Turn the batter into the prepared loaf pan and bake 1 hour to 1 hour and 15 minutes. To test, stick a toothpick in the center; if it comes out dry, the bread is ready. Let cool in pan for 15 minutes and remove. Makes 1 loaf.

Al Forno's Chocolate Bread Pudding

You can prepare this pudding with any type of leftover sweet bread or cake—a zucchini, banana, or nut bread or a coffee, sponge, or angel food cake—or use regular French or Italian, white, or whole wheat bread.

SERVES 8.

> **8 to 10 ¼-inch slices chocolate bread (page 43), or 3 to 4 cups**
> **1-inch cubes leftover bread**
> **3 cups heavy cream**
> **4 eggs**
> **½ cup sugar**

1. Preheat the oven to 350 degrees.

2. Generously butter a shallow six-cup casserole, or a large, long shallow pan.

3. Line the pan with one layer of bread slices.

4. Heat the heavy cream over moderately low heat until hot but not simmering.

5. Beat the eggs with the sugar until well combined. Slowly add the scalded cream and beat until the mixture thickens. Pour the custard mixture over the bread slices.

6. Set the casserole in a pan of hot water and bake for about 45 minutes. The edges should be set and the center should be a bit runny. (The custard will continue to cook after it's been removed from the oven.)

7. Remove the casserole from the water bath and cool on a rack. Serve at room temperature or chilled.

Bread Crumbs

There in the corner of your bread basket or in your freezer are the ends of several loaves of very stale bread. Don't throw them out! Take a small piece of the stale bread and put it in your food processor or blender and process until the bread turns to crumbs. Guess what? You've just made bread crumbs.

If you have a lot of stale bread at one time you can make it all into bread crumbs and store in a well-sealed jar or plastic container. The bread crumbs will keep, covered and refrigerated, for several weeks. I prefer to make the crumbs as I need them, bit by bit.

You can blend the bread until the crumbs are coarsely chopped or process them until they are finely ground. Sprinkle them over fish, poultry, or meat before grilling, coat beef, fish, liver, or poultry before sautéing, mix into stuffings, strew over vegetable dishes, sprinkle into sauces, and so on. Once you see how easy it is to make your own bread crumbs, you won't need to buy the preservative-filled ones found in most grocery stores.

Flavored bread crumbs are also extremely easy to prepare. Simply mix the bread crumbs with an assortment of dried herbs, or mix with finely grated cheese, etc. For example, when broiling lamb chops, I mix 2 tablespoons fresh bread crumbs with about 2 teaspoons chopped fresh rosemary (or 1 teaspoon crumbled dried rosemary), sprinkle the mixture over 2 chops, and broil them until the juices run pink.

Experiment. Why not top a chicken casserole with curry-and-cumin-flavored bread crumbs, or a filet of red snapper with ground-ginger-and-dill-flavored bread crumbs. Grilled eggplant slices are superb topped with garlic, a touch of olive oil, and a mixture of grated Parmesan cheese and bread crumbs and placed under the broiler for a few minutes.

Croutons and Croûtes

Croutons, small cubes of baked bread, are delicious sprinkled into salads and antipasto platters, and on top of stews, soups, and chowders. Croûtes, thin slices of baked bread, can be used for dips and spreads, or added to soups, casseroles, chowders, and stews, with or without melted cheese on top.

There are several ways to make croutons and croûtes. The best, least fatty way is to simply bake small cubes or slices of leftover bread in a moderate oven.

Leftover bread (French, Italian, peasant, white, corn, etc.)
Olive oil (optional)

1. Preheat the oven to 300 degrees.
2. Cut the leftover bread into the shape you desire: croutons are best cut into ½-inch cubes and croûtes should be about ½ to ¾ inch thick.
3. Place the bread on a baking sheet. Bake for about 5 to 10 minutes on each side, or until dried out and lightly browned. If you want the bread to have a flavoring, brush each side with a very light coating of olive oil halfway through baking.
4. Let cool thoroughly and store in an airtight container or plastic bag.

Flavored Croutons

You can make flavored croutons and croûtes by simply following the previous recipe and making a few slight variations:

➤ Peppery Croutons—Halfway through baking, brush the bread lightly with olive oil. Top with freshly ground black pepper and a sprinkling of cayenne pepper.

➤ Cheese Croutons—Halfway through baking, brush one side of the bread liberally with olive oil. Lightly sprinkle one side of the bread with very finely grated cheese (or mixed cheeses) and return to the oven until the cheese is melted and golden brown. Turn the bread over and repeat on the other side.

➤ Garlic Croutons—Halfway through baking, lightly brush the bread with olive oil. When finished baking, rub the bread with a cut clove of garlic and sprinkle with a grinding of black pepper.

➤ Herbed or Spiced Croutons—Halfway through cooking, lightly brush the bread with olive oil and sprinkle with a mixture of fresh or dried herbs or spices—tarragon, rosemary, basil, thyme, oregano, curry powder, cumin, etc.

■■

Italian Garlic Bread
(Bruschetta and Crostini)

This is the original Italian-style garlic bread—pieces of thinly sliced bread grilled and then rubbed with a clove of raw garlic and drizzled with olive oil. Bruschetta is not traditionally made with stale bread; the Italians like the bread to be soft on the inside and grilled on the out. But I've made this successfully using one-, two-, even seven-day-old stale bread. Ideally, this is made with Italian, French, or crusty peasant bread.

Bruschetta and crostini are delicious served in soups, stews, and chowders, or topped with a dip, thin slices of prosciutto and Italian cheese, finely chopped vegetable salad, or a combination of sautéed wild mushrooms. Traditionally these garlic breads are also rubbed with a ripe tomato, with a little of the tomato juice drizzled on at the end.

You can make bruschetta and crostini either by broiling in your oven or by placing the bread over an open fire or barbecue.

To make bruschetta, cut the bread into 1-inch slices; for crostini use ½-inch-thick slices.

MAKES 12 PIECES

12 slices stale, somewhat stale, or very stale bread (see above), cut either 1 inch or ½ inch thick
1 large or 2 small cloves garlic, peeled
Virgin or extra-virgin olive oil

1. Preheat the broiler.
2. Broil the bread about 30 seconds on each side, or until golden brown.
3. Remove and immediately rub the bread with the garlic. Drizzle lightly with the olive oil. The bread can be made ahead and wrapped in foil until ready to use.

GARLIC—ROASTED

Whenever I make a roast—be it chicken, turkey, beef, lamb, pork, or vegetables—I always throw 2, 3, sometimes 4 whole heads of garlic into the bottom of the pan. There are few aromas in this world equal to that of a freshly roasted head of garlic, mingled with the juices from a roast beef or chicken. The garlic becomes permeated by the meat juices and releases its own flavor into the natural "sauce" that forms on the bottom of every roasting pan. I serve 1 or 2 heads of garlic with the roast (to be pulled apart with your hands and sucked out of the garlic skins) and save the remaining ones to use with leftovers.

Of course, you can always skip the roast and simply place a few heads of garlic in a skillet or small roasting pan and drizzle with olive oil, fresh thyme or other herbs, and freshly ground black pepper. Bake at 400 degrees for about 30 minutes to 1 hour, or until soft and near falling apart.

Leftover roasted garlic adds a surprisingly subtle flavor to soups, stocks, stews, and sauces. It makes a wonderful sandwich spread—simply spread the roasted garlic on a piece of dark bread and top with thin slices of roast beef, pork, chicken, or turkey. It's also an unusual addition to an antipasto platter. Serve roasted garlic with croutons (page 47), paper-thin slices of prosciutto, black olives, and fresh figs.

Bread and Herb Stuffing

This is the traditional mixture I use to stuff my Thanksgiving turkey each year. I almost always add fresh oysters as well, but I like to vary the stuffing from year to year. This stuffing is delicious on its own, or it can be the base for several other, richer stuffings; see variations below.

I start collecting leftover bread for stuffing about a week before Thanksgiving. You can use virtually any type of bread you have in the house—whole wheat, corn, herb, cheese, onion-dill, white, etc. The better the quality of bread you use, the better the final flavor of the stuffing.

THE FOLLOWING RECIPE MAKES ABOUT 7½ CUPS, ENOUGH TO STUFF A 10- TO 12-POUND TURKEY, WITH ENOUGH LEFT OVER TO FILL A SMALL CASSEROLE. EVERYONE KNOWS YOU CAN NEVER HAVE TOO MUCH STUFFING.

¼ to ½ pound (1 to 2 sticks) butter
2 medium onions, chopped
4 garlic cloves, minced
6 stalks celery, chopped
2 tablespoons chopped fresh thyme, or 1 tablespoon dried crumbled
2 tablespoons chopped fresh basil, or 1 tablespoon dried crumbled
¾ cup chopped fresh parsley
Freshly ground black pepper
6 cups cubed slightly stale bread

1. In a large skillet, melt 1 stick of butter over moderate heat. Add the onions and sauté for about 5 minutes. Add the garlic, celery, thyme, and basil and cook for an additional 3 to 5 minutes, or until the celery is just beginning to soften. Add half the parsley and a generous grinding of black pepper. Let cook about 30 seconds and cool for about 5 minutes.

2. Place the bread in a large bowl and add the onion/celery mixture and the remaining parsley. Toss thoroughly. If the mixture seems dry, add more melted butter, a touch of milk, or turkey or chicken stock. The overall result should be slightly moist—neither soaking wet nor dry.

3. Stuff into both ends of the turkey and close tightly with skewers or tie with string. Place any leftover stuffing in a lightly oiled casserole, cover, and bake about 35 minutes, or until piping hot. Add any juices from the turkey to the casserole about halfway through baking.

Other Stuffing Variations

▶*Oyster, Bread, and Herb Stuffing:* My father, who *hates* oysters, absolutely loves this stuffing. So don't be turned off because you *think* an oyster stuffing will have a strong fishy flavor. The oysters add a subtle richness and keep the stuffing moist and flavorful.

Add ½ pint shucked oysters, coarsely chopped, with their liquid, to the skillet along with the parsley and pepper in Step 1.

▶*Dried Mushroom, Bread, and Herb Stuffing:* Soak ½ cup dried mushrooms (porcini, shiitake, morels, etc.) in 2 cups hot water for 30 minutes, or until soft. Drain the mushrooms, reserving the liquid, dry thoroughly, and chop coarsely. Add the mushrooms to the bread mixture in Step 2 and moisten with about ½ cup of the strained mushroom liquid.

▶*Sausage, Apple, Bread, and Herb Stuffing:* Remove the casings from 2 links of sweet or spicy Italian sausage and sauté the crumbled sausage meat for 10 minutes in 1 tablespoon olive oil. Remove from the heat and stir in 1½ cups peeled, cubed tart apple. Add to the bread mixture in Step 2.

■■

French Toast

French toast is an ideal way to use stale bread. It acts as a sponge and soaks up the egg mixture and flavorings. Plan on serving at least 2 slices per person.

You can make this French toast plain and simple, with maple syrup and a pat of butter, or fancy it up. Add a tablespoon of bourbon or liqueur to the eggs and then top the French toast with thinly sliced strawberries, kiwi, bananas, grapes, and/or fresh berries and a light dusting of confectioners' sugar. Serve with a pitcher of warm maple syrup on the side.

SERVES 2 TO 3.

3 large eggs
1 tablespoon heavy cream or milk
1 tablespoon maple syrup
$^1/_8$ teaspoon ground cinnamon
$^1/_8$ teaspoon freshly grated nutmeg
Dash of vanilla extract
1 tablespoon bourbon, Grand Marnier, or other liqueur (optional)
4 thick slices or 6 thin slices leftover bread
Butter
Mixed fruit (sliced strawberries, grapes, bananas, berries, etc.)
3 tablespoons confectioners' sugar mixed with $^1/_4$ teaspoon ground
**   cinnamon**

1. In a medium bowl, whisk the eggs with the cream, maple syrup, cinnamon, nutmeg, vanilla, and optional bourbon.

2. Soak the bread in the liquid, one piece at a time, about a minute on each side.

3. In a medium skillet, heat $^1/_2$ tablespoon butter over moderate heat. Cook the bread about $1^1/_2$ minutes, or until golden brown, flip and cook the other side about 30 seconds, or until golden brown. Add more butter if needed when cooking the remaining bread.

Bread and Five-Onion Soup

You would never believe that a hunk of stale bread could produce a soup this thick, rich, and soothing.

SERVES 4 TO 6.

2 tablespoons butter
1 tablespoon olive oil
3 large leeks, cleaned and chopped (about 3 cups)
1 large onion, chopped (about 2 cups)
1/4 cup chopped shallots
2 scallions, chopped
5 garlic cloves, chopped
1 1/2 teaspoons dried thyme, or 3 teaspoons chopped fresh
1/2 cup milk
3/4 cup heavy cream
2 1/2 cups stale, cubed French or Italian bread, crust removed
2 cups chicken stock, preferably homemade (page 193)
Salt
Freshly ground black pepper
Dash Tabasco or other liquid hot pepper sauce (optional)
1/4 cup chopped fresh chives or parsley

1. In a large soup pot, heat the butter and oil over moderately low heat. Add the leeks, onion, shallots, scallions, garlic, and 1 teaspoon of thyme; sauté about 15 minutes, or until softened, stirring frequently.

2. Scald the milk, 1/4 cup of the cream, and the remaining 1/2 teaspoon of thyme.

3. Crumble the bread into a large bowl. Add the scalded milk/cream mixture and mash the bread to form a puree. (The mixture may still be somewhat chunky, which is fine.) Mix in 4 cups water and the chicken stock and add the mixture to the sautéed onions. Raise the heat to high and bring the soup to a boil. Reduce the heat and let the soup simmer partially covered for 20 minutes, stirring occasionally.

4. Transfer the soup to a blender or food processor and blend until smooth. Return the soup back to the pot and add the remaining 1/2 cup cream. Season to taste and sprinkle with the chives or parsley just before serving.

Italian Bread Salad

This is one of the best ways I know to transform stale bread into an interesting salad, full of rich flavors and textures.

Use any type of bread you want with this salad, even a combination of breads. My favorite version is with day-old peasant bread or any kind of sourdough. If the bread isn't completely dry, first place it in a 250-degree oven for a few minutes or toast it slightly.

SERVES 2 TO 4.

> About 1½ cups leftover bread, cut into thick pieces
> Olive oil
> Coarsely ground black pepper
> 3½ tablespoons olive oil
> 3 garlic cloves, minced
> ½ cup diced ripe tomatoes (if you can't find a ripe tomato, simply
>   omit it from the recipe; don't use canned ones), or ⅓ cup
>   marinated chopped sun-dried tomatoes (see The Leftover Pantry)
> 3 scallions, chopped
> ½ cup chopped fresh parsley
> ⅓ cup pine nuts or slivered almonds
> 2½ tablespoons wine vinegar
> 1½ tablespoons milk

1. Place bread on a cookie sheet and drizzle lightly with olive oil on one side and top with a generous coating of black pepper. Place under broiler or in a 500-degree oven for a minute, or until the bread turns golden brown. Repeat on the other side.

2. In a small saucepan, heat the 3½ tablespoons olive oil over moderately low heat. Add the garlic and let simmer about 5 minutes, being careful not to let the garlic brown. Remove from the heat and set aside.

3. Break the bread into bite-sized pieces. Add the garlic oil, tomatoes, scallions, parsley, nuts, vinegar, and milk and toss thoroughly. Taste for seasoning and serve at room temperature.

Bread-and-Herb-Stuffed Tomatoes

This is a recipe to save for August, when perfectly red, ripe, juicy tomatoes are everywhere.

SERVES 5.

> 3 to 4 tablespoons olive oil
> 5 medium ripe tomatoes
> 3 tablespoons coarsely chopped fresh basil, or 3 teaspoons crumbled dried
> 1½ tablespoons finely minced garlic
> 1 teaspoon coarsely chopped fresh sage, or ½ teaspoon crumbled dried
> 1 tablespoon snipped fresh chives
> 1 tablespoon chopped fresh parsley
> 6 tablespoons freshly grated Parmesan cheese
> ¾ cup plus 3 tablespoons bread crumbs (page 46)
> ½ cup pine nuts, chopped almonds or chopped walnuts
> Salt
> Grinding of fresh black pepper

1. Grease a large shallow baking dish with 1 tablespoon of the oil.
2. Cut the tomatoes in half and, using a large spoon, gently scoop out the pulp, being careful to leave the tomato skins intact. You want to scoop out the pulp and leave a shell. Put the tomato shells in the baking dish, and sprinkle a bit of basil inside each and a few drops of olive oil over the basil.
3. Coarsely chop the tomato pulp and place in a large bowl. Add the garlic, the remaining basil, sage, chives, parsley, 4 tablespoons of the cheese, ¾ cup of the bread crumbs, and the pine nuts. Add salt and pepper to taste. Spoon the filling into the tomato shells, packing it down tightly. (The recipe can be made ahead up to this point and refrigerated for several hours or overnight before baking.)
4. Preheat the oven to 350 degrees.
5. Sprinkle the remaining 2 tablespoons of cheese over the tops of the tomatoes, then the remaining 3 tablespoons of bread crumbs. Drizzle with the remaining olive oil and bake for about 15 minutes, or until the tomato shells are soft but not falling apart. Place under the broiler for about 2 minutes, or until the tops of the tomatoes are golden brown and bubbling.

Mushroom, Chive, and Bacon Bread Pudding

The truth is that I don't particularly like sweets. I have always been known as a person who would rather have another piece of grilled chicken than a piece of chocolate cake. With that thought in mind I created a savory version of a traditional bread pudding. The result is a sublime creamy pudding that is a cross between quiche, pizza, and bread pudding.

Use any type of bread you like with this dish. I've found that white or whole wheat bread, rather than a French or Italian loaf, works best. Also, you can easily omit the bacon and make this a vegetarian dish.

SERVES 2 TO 4.

1 tablespoon butter
4 thick strips slab bacon
1 teaspoon olive oil
1 small onion, finely chopped
$1/2$ tablespoon chopped fresh thyme, or $1/4$ teaspoon crumbled dried
3 tablespoons snipped fresh chives
$1/4$ cup dry white wine
$1^1/2$ cups sliced mushrooms
3 tablespoons chopped fresh parsley
Salt
Freshly ground black pepper
4 slices stale white or whole wheat bread
2 large eggs
$1^1/4$ cups milk
$1^1/2$ cups grated cheese (cheddar, Parmesan, Swiss, etc., or
    combination)

1. Preheat the oven to 375 degrees.
2. Grease a medium shallow baking pan or 4- to 5-cup soufflé dish with the butter.
3. In a medium skillet, cook the bacon slowly over moderately low heat. Drain on paper towels and discard all but 1 teaspoon of the bacon fat.
4. Heat the remaining bacon fat and the olive oil over moderate heat. (If you're preparing this without bacon, simply heat 2 teaspoons olive oil.) Sauté the onion with the thyme and half the chives for 5 minutes, or until softened but not brown. Raise the heat to high and add the wine and the mushrooms, stirring well. Let simmer about 5 minutes, or until the wine has almost completely evaporated and the mushrooms are soft. Remove from the heat. Crumble the bacon and add to the

mushroom mixture along with the parsley. Season with salt and pepper. Let cool.

5. Remove the crusts from the bread and slice in half. Line the bottom of the baking pan, using the crusts if needed to fill in any spaces not covered.

6. Whisk the eggs with the milk and the remaining chives. Season to taste with salt and pepper.

7. Place the mushroom mixture over the bread and top with the cheese. Pour the custard on top and cover with aluminum foil. Bake for 15 minutes. Remove the foil and bake an additional 10 to 15 minutes, or until the cheese is bubbling and the custard is set. Serve hot, warm, or room temperature.

■■

Creamed Mushrooms on Toast

The title of this recipe is deceptive; it sounds like an old childhood favorite, but actually this dish is quite rich, grown-up, and elegant. Serve as an hors d'oeuvre, first course, lunch dish, or a sinful midnight snack.

SERVES 2 TO 4.

2 slices stale firm-textured white bread
4 tablespoons butter
³/₄ pound mushrooms, quartered
¹/₄ cup Cognac or brandy
1 cup heavy cream
Salt
Freshly ground black pepper
Watercress sprigs

1. Preheat the oven to 350 degrees.

2. Remove the crust and cut the bread in half diagonally. Toast in the oven about 2 to 3 minutes on each side, or until golden brown. (The bread should be very dried out so it will act as a platform for the sauce and soak up some of its creaminess.)

3. In a large skillet, melt the butter over moderate heat. Add the mushrooms and sauté about 3 minutes. Add the Cognac and cook another 2 minutes, or until slightly reduced. Add the cream and simmer until the cream is reduced by half, about 8 minutes. Season with salt and pepper.

4. Spoon the mushroom mixture evenly over the toast, and garnish with the watercress sprigs.

SEE ALSO:

3

FISH

MASTER RECIPES

LEFTOVER RECIPES

MASTER RECIPE:

SWORDFISH

This is an unusual way of cooking swordfish. The fish is marinated in milk, which tenderizes and flavors. The milk blends with the natural fish juices and creates a delicious sauce.

SERVES 2 TO 3.

>   1 pound swordfish, about 1 to 1 1/2 inches thick
>   3/4 cup milk
>   1 1/2 tablespoons butter
>   1 teaspoon Dijon mustard
>   1 tablespoon drained capers
>   1 tablespoon fresh lemon juice
>   1 1/2 teaspoons chopped fresh thyme, or 1/2 teaspoon crumbled dried

1. Place the swordfish in a shallow ovenproof casserole and pour the milk over it. Marinate for 1 hour or up to 24 hours in the refrigerator.
2. Preheat the oven to 350 degrees.
3. In a small saucepan melt the butter over moderately low heat. Whisk in the mustard, capers, lemon juice, and thyme and cook about 3 to 4 minutes, or until slightly thickened and bubbling.
4. Spoon the butter sauce over the swordfish and bake for about 15 minutes, or until just tender.
5. Place the fish under the broiler for about 3 to 5 minutes, or until golden brown and bubbling.

MASTER RECIPE:

POACHED WHOLE SALMON

Throughout New England, tradition dictates that a proper Fourth of July meal includes poached whole salmon, fresh peas, and boiled new potatoes. No matter where you live, don't wait for a national holiday to prepare this salmon. It will be well appreciated anytime.

This recipe is adapted from *American Cooking: New England* by Jonathan Norton Leonard (Time-Life Books, 1970).

SERVES 8 TO 10.

(continued)

The Fish Broth:
1 pound fish trimmings (head, tail, and bones of any firm-fleshed fish)
1½ cups thinly sliced onions
1 cup thinly sliced celery
½ cup thinly sliced carrots
2 sprigs of fresh parsley
2 tablespoons fresh lemon juice
1 bay leaf
1 tablespoon whole black peppercorns
1 teaspoon salt

The Fish and Dill-Lemon Butter:
1 (6- to 7-pound) salmon, cleaned, with head and tail*
Lemon wedges
1 cucumber, peeled and thinly sliced
Fresh dill sprigs
8 tablespoons (1 stick) butter
2 tablespoons minced fresh dill
1 tablespoon fresh lemon juice

1. Make the fish broth: Combine the fish trimmings, 4 quarts of water, the onions, celery, carrots, parsley, lemon juice, bay leaf, peppercorns, and salt in a large saucepan set over high heat. Bring to a boil, reduce the heat, and simmer gently, partially covered, for 25 minutes. Strain the broth into a 12-quart fish poacher or a roasting pan large enough to hold the salmon. Cover and bring to a boil.

2. Meanwhile, gently rinse the salmon in cold running water. Wrap it in a double thickness of cheesecloth, leaving about 6 inches of cloth at each end to serve as handles for lifting the fish in and out of the simmering broth. Twist the ends of the cheesecloth and tie each end with string.

3. Place the fish on the rack of the poacher and lower into the poacher or the roasting pan. The stock should completely cover the fish; if it doesn't, add water. Cover the poacher, reduce the heat to a gentle simmer, and poach for about 30 minutes, or until the salmon feels firm to the touch.

4. Remove the salmon from the broth and take off the cheesecloth. Peel off the salmon's skin using a small, sharp knife. Gently flip the salmon and remove the skin on the other side. Place on a serving platter and surround with the lemon wedges, cucumber slices, and dill sprigs.

*If the salmon doesn't fit in the pan or poacher, remove the head.

5. Prepare the dill-lemon butter: Place the butter in a small saucepan over moderate heat and melt. Add the dill and lemon juice, and simmer 1 minute, or until warmed through. Serve the warm butter alongside the salmon.

MASTER RECIPE:

BAKED BLUEFISH WITH TOMATOES, ONIONS, AND BASIL

SERVES 2 TO 3.

2 tablespoons olive oil
1 pound fresh bluefish filet
2 small garlic cloves, very thinly sliced
1 medium onion, very thinly sliced
3 tablespoons chopped fresh basil, or 1 tablespoon crumbled dried
1 large ripe tomato or 10 cherry tomatoes, very thinly sliced
Freshly ground black pepper
⅓ cup dry white wine

1. Preheat the oven to 350 degrees.
2. Grease the bottom of a large ovenproof skillet with 1 tablespoon of the oil. Place the bluefish in the skillet, skin side down. Insert the garlic into the flesh of the fish. Top with the onion, half the basil, tomatoes, and pepper. Pour the wine over the fish and sprinkle the remaining basil on top. Drizzle the remaining tablespoon of olive oil over the top and bake for 10 to 15 minutes, depending on the thickness of the fish, or until tender and flaky when tested with a fork.
3. Place under the broiler for a minute or two, or until brown and bubbling.

MASTER RECIPE:

BROILED JAPANESE-STYLE TUNA

Filet of salmon also works well with this recipe. If you have a larger filet (up to 2 pounds), add double the amount of soy sauce, sake, ginger, and sesame oil. You can broil the fish or wrap it in foil and barbecue.

SERVES 2 TO 3.

 1½ teaspoons vegetable or safflower oil
 8 scallions, cut into 2½-inch pieces
 1 pound filet of tuna or salmon
 1½ tablespoons light soy sauce or tamari
 1½ tablespoons sake, Chinese rice wine, or dry sherry
 1½ teaspoons grated fresh ginger
 1 teaspoon sesame oil

1. Oil the bottom of an ovenproof skillet or shallow baking dish. Place the scallion pieces in a thin layer on the bottom of the skillet. Place the fish on the scallions and top with the soy, sake, ginger, and sesame oil. Marinate 30 minutes, or cover and refrigerate overnight.

2. Preheat the broiler. Grill the fish for about 8 to 12 minutes, depending on the thickness of the filet, or until tender when tested with a fork. If you want to barbecue the fish, wrap it in a double layer of aluminum foil and place over the hot coals for about 10 minutes, or until tender.

MASTER RECIPE:

BROILED SCALLOPS

Try to find really fresh bay scallops for this recipe, as they are considerably smaller, sweeter, and more tender than sea scallops. If you are using large sea scallops, cut them in half horizontally.

This is a simple broil, but if you like you could top the scallops with 3 tablespoons coarse bread crumbs mixed with 1½ tablespoons freshly grated Parmesan cheese during the last minute of broiling.

Serve with broiled tomatoes, steamed rice, and lemon wedges.

SERVES 2 TO 3.

1 pound fresh bay scallops
1½ tablespoons minced garlic
2 tablespoons butter, cut into cubes
Paprika
Freshly ground black pepper
Salt
⅓ cup minced fresh parsley
Lemon wedges

1. Preheat the broiler.
2. Wash the scallops under cold running water and dry thoroughly. Place in a medium ovenproof skillet or shallow casserole. Scatter the garlic over the scallops and dot with the butter cubes. Sprinkle liberally with the paprika and pepper and just a touch of salt, if desired.
3. Broil for 6 to 8 minutes, depending on the size of the scallops, until golden brown. Remove from the broiler, sprinkle with the parsley, and serve directly from the skillet surrounded by lemon wedges.

MASTER RECIPE:

SCALLOPS POACHED IN ORANGE JUICE

This is an extremely light, refreshing way of preparing fresh bay or sea scallops, ideal for summer salads. Try mixing the poached scallops with chopped orange segments, ripe tomato wedges, and chopped parsley, and tossing with a vinaigrette flavored with a tablespoon or two of the orange poaching liquid.

You can also serve these scallops cold, accompanied by orange and lemon wedges and a homemade mayonnaise or tartar sauce (page 238).

SERVES 4.

1 cup fresh bay or sea scallops
2 cups orange juice, preferably freshly squeezed
Orange and lemon wedges

1. Wash the scallops under cold running water and dry thoroughly.
2. Bring the orange juice to a gentle boil in a medium skillet. Reduce the heat and add the scallops. Poach for 2 to 4 minutes for bay scallops and 6 to 8 minutes for the larger sea scallops. Scallops should be *almost* firm to the touch. Remove the scallops and serve with orange and lemon wedges. Serve warm or cold.

MASTER RECIPE:

BOILED LOBSTER

Cooking a live lobster couldn't be easier. But there are a few "musts": the lobster must be alive and squirming, and the water must be at a rolling boil.

Serve with melted butter, lemon wedges, Tabasco sauce, warm biscuits or dinner rolls, homemade coleslaw, baked potatoes, and lots of large napkins.

SERVES 2.

2 (1¼- to 1½-pound) lobsters
Salt or seaweed

1. Bring a large pot of water to a rolling boil. Add a large pinch of salt. (If you have access to fresh seaweed, add a few strips instead of the salt.) Add the lobsters to the pot *back first* (so the juices get caught in the shell and not lost in the pot). Cover and let boil about 12 to 15 minutes, depending on the size of the lobster.

2. To test for doneness, simply pull one of the legs; if it pulls off easily, the lobster is ready. Drain and serve.

MASTER RECIPE:

BOILED SHRIMP

Boiling shrimp is a surprisingly simple, quick process. I've never quite understood why people are willing to pay fish shops an extra $5 to $10 to cook and shell the shrimp.

Salt
Shrimp

1. Bring a large pot of lightly salted water to a rolling boil. Add shrimp and boil; small shrimp should take about 3 minutes, while medium to large shrimp take about 5 minutes to turn pink and tender. Remove and place the shrimp in a bowl of cold water to stop the cooking process.

2. When cool, peel the shells off. I generally don't bother deveining the shrimp. However, if you insist, make a small slit down the back of the shrimp and gently pull out the black vein from the back with the tip of a small sharp knife. Refrigerate until ready to use.

3. Serve with a spicy cocktail sauce, an herb-flavored mayonnaise, pesto, or simply a bowl of lemon and lime wedges.

Swordfish Salad with Roasted Peppers
and Anchovy Vinaigrette

This salad is delicious made with any firm, full-flavored fish—salmon, halibut, mahi-mahi, tuna, etc. You could also use 1/2 pound of large, thinly sliced sea scallops. It's a particularly colorful dish (especially if you can get your hands on red *and* yellow peppers) that makes an elegant lunch entrée or first course. Serve with a warm loaf of crusty bread and crisp, dry white wine. Follow with a simple pasta dish or grilled veal or lamb chops.

SERVES 2.

1 large red bell pepper
1 large yellow or green bell pepper
1 tablespoon minced garlic
1 1/2 teaspoons anchovy oil (drained from the can)
1 1/2 tablespoons red wine vinegar
2 1/2 tablespoons olive oil
Freshly ground black pepper
5 to 6 anchovy filets
About 1/2 pound cooked swordfish, cut on the diagonal into thin
    slices

1. Preheat the broiler.
2. Place the peppers on a piece of aluminum foil and cook under the broiler for about 4 minutes on each side, or until completely charred. Remove and wrap in the foil for about 3 minutes. Immediately peel the charred skin off the peppers; cut into thick slices, removing the inside seeds and ribbing.
3. Combine the garlic and anchovy oil in a small bowl. Add the vinegar, olive oil, and pepper.
4. Place the pepper strips around the outside of a medium serving platter, alternating red and yellow (or green) strips. Drape the anchovy filets over the peppers, and arrange the fish slices in the middle of the platter. Pour the vinaigrette over the fish and peppers and marinate at room temperature for at least 10 minutes, and up to several hours refrigerated, before serving.

Shrimp, Pea, and Pasta Salad

This is a delicious salad to make in the early summer when you have some leftover cooked shrimp on hand and fresh peas are available. You can use any type of pasta shapes; I particularly like small shells. Leftover cooked pasta can also be used. If you cook the pasta, peas, and hard-boiled eggs and prepare the mayonnaise ahead, the salad can be put together just a few minutes before serving.

SERVES 4.

1 cup raw or cooked peas
2 eggs
$1/2$ pound small shaped pasta
1 cup cooked shrimp
1 cup mayonnaise
2 tablespoons dry white wine
Salt
Freshly ground black pepper
$1/2$ cup minced fresh parsley
$1/3$ cup thinly sliced scallions
$1/4$ cup chopped pimiento
1 tablespoon fresh lemon juice
1 tablespoon chopped fresh chives

1. If the peas are not exceptionally fresh and young, cook them in a pot of boiling water until just tender. Drain, refresh under cold running water, and drain again. Set aside.

2. Cook the eggs in a pot of simmering water until hard-boiled. Drain, and soak in cold water. Peel the eggs, chop, and set aside.

3. Bring a large pot of water to a boil. Boil the pasta until just tender, about 8 to 10 minutes. Rinse under cold running water, drain, and place in a large serving bowl.

4. Chop $1/3$ cup of the shrimp. Add it to the container of a blender or food processor with the cooked eggs, mayonnaise, wine, a pinch of salt, and pepper, and blend until smooth. (The recipe can be made ahead up to this point.)

5. Cut the remaining shrimp into small pieces. Gently stir in the cooked peas, parsley, scallions, pimiento, and lemon juice. Gently mix in the mayonnaise and the pasta. Top with the shrimp and chives and serve chilled.

Oriental Fish and Green Bean Salad

This salad works particularly well with leftover broiled tuna, swordfish, or any other thick, firm-fleshed fish. Poached salmon also works well.

SERVES 2.

¹/₂ pound green beans, ends trimmed
About ¹/₂ pound broiled tuna (see headnote)
³/₄ tablespoon minced fresh ginger
¹/₃ cup mirin (sweet Japanese rice wine) or plum wine
¹/₃ cup soy sauce
¹/₂ tablespoon sesame oil

1. In a large pot of boiling, salted water, cook beans until just tender, about 3 to 5 minutes. Refresh beans under cold running water and drain.

2. Remove any skin from the fish, and cut on the diagonal into thick slices.

3. To prepare the sauce, combine the ginger, mirin, soy sauce, and sesame oil in a small saucepan, and cook over medium heat for about 4 to 5 minutes.

4. Place the fish in the center of the plate and surround with the beans. Pour the sauce over the beans and fish and let sit for at least 15 minutes and up to several hours. Serve at room temperature.

■■■

Mediterranean-Style Tuna and Bean Salad

This is a variation of the classic Salade Niçoise, using slices of leftover cooked fresh tuna (or any other firm-fleshed, flavorful fish). You could also use canned tuna in this recipe. This salad can also be fleshed out with quartered hard-boiled eggs, thin strips of prosciutto, and edible flowers such as nasturtium. Serve with Italian garlic bread (page 48) or buttered toast.

SERVES 2 TO 4.

> 1 large clove garlic, minced
> 1 teaspoon salt
> 3 tablespoons red wine vinegar
> 1 1/2 tablespoons balsamic vinegar or fresh lemon juice
> 7 tablespoons olive oil
> 2 1/2 tablespoons chopped fresh thyme or parsley
> Freshly ground black pepper
> 4 cups assorted greens, cut into bite-sized pieces (arugula, red leaf
>   lettuce, watercress, etc.)
> 1 to 1 1/2 cups thin, bite-sized pieces cooked tuna (or other firm-
>   fleshed fish), or a 6 1/2-ounce can tuna, drained
> 1 1/2 cups cooked cannellini beans (page 253), or a 19-ounce can,
>   thoroughly drained
> 1 cup 2-inch pieces cooked green beans (optional)
> 1 cup tiny black olives, pitted
> 2 tablespoons snipped fresh chives or minced fresh parsley
> 2 scallions, finely chopped

1. In a large wooden salad bowl, crush the minced garlic with the salt using the back of a spoon or fork. Add the vinegars and whisk in the olive oil. Add 1 tablespoon of the thyme (or parsley) and a generous grinding of fresh pepper.

2. Add the greens to the salad bowl. Arrange the fish, white beans, green beans, and olives on top. Sprinkle with the chives, scallions, and remaining thyme. Toss well before serving.

■■

Fish Stew

This fish stew can be made with any type of leftover broiled fish—halibut, scrod, swordfish, tuna, bluefish, scallops, etc. The stew will be particularly flavorful if you also throw in a small raw (or cooked) lobster chopped into pieces or a dozen raw clams or mussels. Serve with a warm loaf of crusty bread and cannellini beans sautéed with onions, parsley, and garlic.

SERVES 2 TO 4.

1½ tablespoons olive oil
2 medium onions, chopped
3 cloves garlic, chopped
1½ tablespoons chopped fresh thyme, or 1 teaspoon crumbled dried
1 tablespoon chopped fresh rosemary, or 1 teaspoon crumbled dried
½ cup chopped fresh Italian parsley
1½ cups thinly sliced summer squash
1½ cups thinly sliced zucchini
2 cups chopped fresh, very ripe tomatoes, with juice, or 2 cups
　　chopped canned plum tomatoes
1 cup dry white wine
1½ cups peeled, cubed cooked potatoes
2½ cups cubed broiled fish
1 cooked or raw lobster, cut into pieces (optional)
12 clams or mussels (optional)*
½ cup fish broth or clam juice**

1. In a soup pot or casserole, heat the oil over moderate heat. Add the onions and half each of the garlic, thyme, rosemary, and parsley and sauté about 5 minutes, or until softened but not brown. Add the squash and zucchini slices, raise the heat to high, and sauté about 2 minutes, stirring constantly. Add the tomatoes and their juice and the wine and bring to a boil.

2. Reduce the heat and add the potatoes, fish, shellfish (if using), and broth or clam juice. (Only add the fish broth if you are not adding any

---

*If using clams or mussels, soak them in a bowl of cold water with 1 tablespoon cornmeal for about 15 minutes. The clams will open their shells to eat the cornmeal and lose their excess sand and dirt. Rinse well before cooking.

**If you use a lobster and/or clams or mussels you don't need to add the broth or clam juice.

shellfish to the stew.) Stir in the remaining garlic, thyme, and rosemary. Cover partially, and let simmer about 15 minutes, or until the clams and/or mussels have opened, the lobster has turned bright red, and the soup has thickened slightly. Just before serving, sprinkle with the remaining parsley.

■■

Gingered Bluefish Pâté

Bluefish, an oily and flavorful fish, is relatively inexpensive on the East Coast. You can use the leftovers for a salad (mixed with mayonnaise or tossed with a simple vinaigrette) or make this quick, simple pâté.

Serve it with crackers, buttered toast points, or a crudité platter, or use a tablespoonful to top off a broiled swordfish, tuna, or salmon steak.

This recipe works well with any leftover, full-flavored, oily fish.

SERVES 2 TO 4.

½ pound cooked bluefish*
4 ounces cream cheese
1 tablespoon fresh lemon juice
1 tablespoon chopped fresh ginger
About 1 teaspoon Tabasco or other liquid hot pepper sauce
2 scallions, chopped
Salt
Freshly ground black pepper
2 scallions, cut in half lengthwise and then in quarters
½ lemon, cut into paper-thin slices
½ cup thinly sliced smoked bluefish (optional)

1. Place the bluefish, cream cheese, lemon juice, ginger, and Tabasco in the container of a food processor and process until smooth. (This can also be done in a blender in small batches.) Add the chopped scallions and process for just a second or two; you don't want the scallions to be pureed. Taste for seasoning and add salt and pepper as needed.

2. Place pâté in a small serving bowl or a ramekin and garnish with scallions, lemon slices, and smoked bluefish if available.

*If you've used the recipe for baked bluefish (page 63), add any remaining tomatoes and onions along with the fish.

Washington Street Eatery's Fish Cakes

These light and flavorful fish cakes are from Lu Ann Paquette, owner of the Washington Street Eatery, a wonderful little restaurant in the historic district of Portsmouth, New Hampshire. I've adapted the recipe to use cooked fish and cooked potatoes.

This recipe calls for cod, but you can prepare these cakes with just about any cooked or smoked fish—bluefish, flounder, salmon, crabmeat, bass, snapper, etc. Serve for breakfast with fried eggs and toast, or for lunch and dinner, along with homemade tartar sauce and lemon wedges.

SERVES 4; MAKES ABOUT 8 CAKES.

  1 pound cooked cod or other fish (see headnote)
  2 medium cooked potatoes
  2 large eggs
  2 scallions, chopped
  1½ tablespoons minced fresh parsley
  1½ tablespoons Worcestershire sauce
  1 tablespoon Dijon mustard
  ¾ tablespoon grated fresh ginger, or 1 teaspoon powdered
  2 dashes Tabasco or other liquid hot pepper sauce
  Salt
  Freshly ground black pepper
  1 cup cornmeal
  Vegetable oil
  Tartar sauce (page 238)
  Lemon wedges

1. In a large bowl, mash the fish and potatoes together. (It's best to do this by hand with a masher or a fork or the back of a spoon. A food processor or blender will puree the mixture too much.) Add all the remaining ingredients, *except* the cornmeal and vegetable oil, and mix well.

2. Place the cornmeal on a large plate. Using your hands, form the mixture into 3-inch patties. Coat the cakes thoroughly with the cornmeal.

3. Heat a small amount of oil in a large skillet over moderately high heat. Sauté the cakes about 3 to 4 minutes, flip to the other side, and press down on the cakes with the spatula. Sauté another 3 minutes, or until golden on each side. Serve with tartar sauce and lemon wedges on the side.

LOBSTER (OR SEAFOOD) SALAD

Leftover lobster is not exactly what you'd call a common problem. However, there is the rare occasion when you cook too much or can't finish the entire lobster in a restaurant. (We were at a "lobster shack" on the coast of Maine and the daily special was three 1½-pound lobsters for $12. We couldn't resist. We also couldn't finish them.)

If you find yourself in the fortunate position of having too many crustaceans around, there are several solutions. Use the meat for a lobster stew, add it to a fish stew or chowder, or make a simple lobster salad. You can also use this recipe for cooked shrimp, crab, salmon, and scallops (if using large sea scallops cut them in half horizontally). It's also irresistible with a mixture of cooked fish.

Cut the lobster into small chunks. Mix in homemade mayonnaise to taste, the juice of ½ lemon, a grinding of fresh black pepper, and a tablespoon or two of tiny capers. Taste for seasoning and serve on tender buttercrunch lettuce with a warm baguette, hard rolls, or soft egg rolls.

Chinese-Style Shrimp, Celery, and Ginger Pancakes with a Soy-Ginger-Vinegar Dipping Sauce

These pancakes can also be made with cooked scallops or bits of any firm cooked fish.

SERVES 4.

The Shrimp:

1 cup cooked shrimp, halved or quartered, or 1 cup scallops or
    bite-sized pieces cooked firm-fleshed fish
2 teaspoons soy sauce
1 teaspoon sesame oil
1 tablespoon minced fresh ginger

The Dipping Sauce:

$^1/_4$ cup thinly sliced scallions
$^1/_4$ cup light soy sauce or tamari
2 tablespoons balsamic or red wine vinegar
1 teaspoon minced fresh ginger
1 teaspoon sesame oil

The Pancakes:

$^1/_3$ cup flour
$^1/_2$ teaspoon double-acting baking powder
$^1/_2$ teaspoon salt
2 eggs
Freshly ground black pepper
$^1/_4$ cup finely chopped scallions
$1^1/_2$ teaspoons peanut oil
$^1/_2$ cup julienne strips celery
1 tablespoon julienne strips fresh ginger
About 2 tablespoons peanut or vegetable oil

1. Prepare the shrimp: In a medium bowl, mix the shrimp with the soy sauce, sesame oil, and ginger; marinate in the refrigerator, covered, for about 1 hour.

2. Prepare the dipping sauce: Combine all the ingredients in a medium bowl and set aside.

3. Prepare the pancake batter: Sift the flour with the baking powder and salt into a large bowl. Make a well in the center of the flour and add the eggs. Whisk until smooth. Stir in the pepper, scallions, oil, celery, ginger, and the marinated shrimp along with the marinade.

4. Heat 1 tablespoon of the oil in a large skillet over high heat. When the oil is hot, add a heaping tablespoon of the batter (making sure to include at least 1 or 2 pieces of shrimp or fish) to the skillet. Cook about 1½ minutes and flip. Cook an additional minute on the other side, or until golden brown. Keep warm in a low oven and serve immediately with the dipping sauce. Makes about 10 pancakes.

■■■

Stir-Fried Scallops with Vegetables and Black Bean Sauce

Serve with steamed rice or pasta.

SERVES 2.

1½ tablespoons safflower or peanut oil
4 tablespoons chopped onion
1 cup julienne strips zucchini
6 asparagus spears, cut into 2-inch-long pieces, with the tough stems discarded, or ½ cup chopped leeks
½ cup chopped scallions
2 tablespoons Chinese fermented black beans, rinsed and chopped
1 cup sliced cooked scallops, about 7 to 8 ounces
4 tablespoons Chinese rice wine or dry sherry
2 tablespoons soy sauce
2 tablespoons butter

1. In a wok or a large skillet heat the oil over high heat. Add the onion and sauté about 1 minute, stirring constantly to prevent burning. Add the zucchini and asparagus and sauté 30 seconds.

2. Add the scallions, black beans, and scallops and stir. Add the rice wine and soy sauce and bring to a boil. Reduce heat and simmer about 2 minutes, or until slightly thickened. Remove from the heat and stir in the butter.

Stir-Fried Lime Shrimp Served on a Bed of Bok Choy

This dish can also be made with leftover lobster or crabmeat. Serve with steamed rice and lime wedges.

SERVES 1 TO 2.

1 small, tender bok choy, or ½ medium head iceberg lettuce
½ tablespoon peanut oil
½ tablespoon thin julienne strips fresh ginger
2 scallions, sliced lengthwise and cut into 2-inch pieces
1½ tablespoons fresh lime juice
½ teaspoon sesame oil
½ tablespoon soy sauce
1 tablespoon finely chopped fresh coriander
About ½ pound shelled cooked shrimp
1 lime, cut into wedges

1. Place bok choy or lettuce leaves in a steam basket or tray and steam over boiling water for 3 to 6 minutes, or until tender but not limp. (The greens should still have a slight bite to them.) Remove from the water, drain, and cover to keep warm.

2. Heat a wok or skillet over moderate heat. Add the peanut oil and sauté the ginger and scallions for 1 to 2 minutes. Add the lime juice, sesame oil, soy sauce, and half the coriander; let simmer about a minute. Add the shrimp and cook just long enough to let them get warm.

3. Place the bok choy on a serving plate. Place the shrimp and sauce in the center. Sprinkle the remaining coriander on top and garnish with the lime wedges.

Spicy Chinese Noodles with Shrimp

This is my adaptation of the Sichuan dish *dan dan* noodles—a dish of wheat noodles swimming in a wonderfully spicy chile sauce. The addition of cooked shrimp, scallions, and chopped coriander makes it a complete meal. You could also add bits of cooked crab, lobster, or scallops.

SERVES 2 TO 3.

1 tablespoon peanut or vegetable oil
2 teaspoons minced garlic
2 teaspoons minced fresh ginger
1 1/2 tablespoons soy sauce
1 tablespoon Chinese rice wine or dry sherry
1/2 to 1 tablespoon Chinese chile paste*
1 1/2 tablespoons tahini
2 tablespoons Chinese fermented black beans, rinsed and chopped (optional)
2 cups chicken stock (page 193)
1/2 pound flat thin wheat noodles
3/4 cup cooked shrimp, cut into quarters if they're large and in half if small, or bits of cooked lobster or crabmeat (see headnote)
3 scallions, thinly sliced
1 1/2 tablespoons chopped fresh coriander (optional)

1. In a wok or a medium skillet, heat the oil over moderate heat. Add the garlic and ginger and sauté for about 20 seconds. Add the soy sauce, rice wine, chile paste, tahini, and black beans and stir until smooth. Add the chicken stock and let the sauce come to a boil. Reduce the heat and let simmer until the noodles are ready.

2. Bring a large pot of water to a boil. Add the noodles and cook about 2 to 6 minutes, depending on the thickness of the noodles, until soft. Drain.

3. Add the shrimp to the warm sauce and heat for just a few seconds. Divide the noodles among 2 or 3 serving bowls. Spoon the sauce over the noodles evenly and top with the sliced scallions and coriander.

*More than 1/2 tablespoon will make the sauce dangerously spicy.

■■

Salmon, Spinach, and Asparagus Tart

This is a luscious, savory tart that can include any number of leftover ingredients. I put this together one day when I had some leftover poached salmon, a bit of cooked spinach, and a few spears of cooked asparagus. I've also made it using cooked filet of sole, spinach, and zucchini; or thinly sliced cooked scallops and sorrel. Check the refrigerator.

SERVES 4 TO 6.

The Pastry:
1 1/2 cups flour
1 teaspoon salt
12 tablespoons (1 1/2 sticks) butter
About 3 tablespoons ice-cold water

The Filling:
2 tablespoons olive oil
2 large onions, thinly sliced
4 shallots or garlic cloves, thinly sliced
1 1/2 tablespoons chopped fresh thyme, or 1 teaspoon crumbled dried
Salt
Freshly ground black pepper
About 1 cup cooked spinach (optional), finely chopped
1 1/2 cups heavy cream
1/3 cup freshly grated Parmesan cheese
1 1/2 cups bite-sized pieces cooked salmon, sole, cod, or other white
    fish; or shrimp, crabmeat, or lobster
12 asparagus spears, cooked until just tender

1. Make the pastry: Sift the flour and salt into a bowl. Cut the butter into small pieces and, using two knives, work it into the flour until the mixture resembles bread crumbs. Make a well in the center and add enough water to make the dough come together into a ball. Wrap and chill for at least 1 hour. Roll out the dough on a floured surface and fit into a 9-inch tart pan with a removable bottom. Chill the pastry while you prepare the filling.
2. Preheat the oven to 400 degrees.
3. Prepare the filling: Heat the oil in a large skillet over low heat. Add the onions and shallots or garlic and cook for about 20 minutes,

until golden brown. (Don't try to cook them faster over a higher heat or they won't get that wonderful sweet, caramelized flavor.) Add the thyme, salt and pepper to taste, and the optional cooked spinach. Add the cream and let simmer for about 5 minutes, or until slightly thickened. Remove from the heat and gently fold in the grated cheese. Pour the filling into the crust and top with the pieces of fish. Arrange the cooked asparagus over the fish, creating a circular pattern. (You may have to trim the asparagus to make it fit in the pastry.)

4. Place the tart on a baking tray (or cookie sheet), put in the oven, and lower the heat to 325 degrees. Bake for 1 hour. To test for doneness, the tart should be just set; a toothpick inserted in the center will be almost dry. Remove from the oven and let sit 10 minutes before serving. The tart will finish setting as it cools.

SEE ALSO:

MEXICAN STEAK SANDWICH WITH AVOCADO CREAM   22
Substitute 8 thin slices cooked sole, salmon, or other firm-fleshed fish, at room temperature, for the steak.

SPRING STEAK AND ASPARAGUS SALAD   26
Substitute about 10 thin slices cooked swordfish, bluefish, tuna, or salmon for the steak.

SPINACH LINGUINE WITH LAMB, LEEKS, AND ROASTED RED PEPPERS   106
Substitute 1/2 to 3/4 cup chopped or thinly sliced cooked shrimp, crab, lobster, or poached salmon for the lamb.

LAMB-AND-RICE-STUFFED ZUCCHINI   109
Substitute 1 cup very finely chopped cooked shrimp or shredded poached salmon for the lamb, add a touch of lemon juice, a few chopped almonds or pine nuts, and substitute 1 teaspoon crumbled dried thyme for the cinnamon.

CURRIED RICE WITH RAISINS AND SLIVERED ALMONDS   131
Add 1/2 cup cooked shrimp to the rice and heat for 1 minute.

FRENCH-STYLE POTATO SALAD   139
Add 1/2 cup chopped cooked shrimp or salmon to the salad.

THAI COCONUT AND CHICKEN SOUP   198
Substitute 1 cup chopped cooked shrimp or firm-fleshed fish for the chicken.

FLORIDA DUCK SALAD WITH AVOCADO-GRAPEFRUIT
    MAYONNAISE   202
Substitute 1 cup cooked shrimp, sliced lengthwise, for the duck.

Substitute 1 to 1½ cups thinly sliced cooked shrimp, poached salmon, or firm-fleshed fish for the chicken.
Substitute ½ to 1 cup chopped cooked shrimp for the duck.
Substitute 1½ cups thinly sliced cooked shrimp for the chicken.

4

LAMB

MASTER RECIPES

LEFTOVER RECIPES

MASTER RECIPE:

ROAST LEG OF LAMB

Don't make the mistake I always do when roasting a leg of lamb by invit-
ing too many people to dinner; there won't be anything left over. And, as
far as I'm concerned, leftover leg of lamb is almost better than the hot
roast.

Serve with roast potatoes, garlic, and onions, pureed spinach, and a
watercress, red onion, and mandarin orange salad dressed with a piquant
mustard vinaigrette.

A 6-POUND LAMB WILL SERVE 8 TO 10 PEOPLE.

The Lamb:

1 (6- to 9-pound) leg of lamb, trimmed of any excess fat
6 to 8 large garlic cloves, peeled and cut into thin slivers
3 tablespoons olive oil
¹/₂ cup red or white wine
2¹/₂ tablespoons balsamic, sherry, or red wine vinegar
4 to 5 sprigs fresh rosemary, or 1 teaspoon crumbled dried
Freshly ground black pepper
Watercress for garnish

The Gravy:

About 1 to 2 tablespoons flour
Boiling water, stock, or wine
Salt
Freshly ground black pepper

1. Place the lamb in a large roasting pan. Make thin X's in the skin
of the lamb and insert the garlic. Coat the top, sides, and bottom of the
meat with the olive oil. Pour the wine and vinegar over the lamb and
scatter the rosemary and a generous grinding of pepper on top. Cover
and let marinate in the refrigerator for several hours or overnight.
2. Preheat the oven to 450 degrees.
3. Put the lamb in the oven and bake 15 minutes. Reduce the heat
to 350 degrees and roast about 10 to 12 minutes per pound, or until the
meat reaches an internal temperature of 140 degrees. This will produce
meat that is pink; if you like your lamb well done keep it in the oven an
additional 5 minutes per pound.
4. Remove the meat to a large serving platter. Garnish with

(continued)

watercress. Let the meat rest while you make the gravy.

5. Degrease the pan juices, then heat the pan on top of the stove, scraping up any bits and pieces that cling to the bottom. Add 1 to 2 tablespoons of flour to the juices, depending on the amount of juice you have, and stir to thicken. If the gravy gets too thick, add a touch of water, lamb or chicken stock, or wine. Season the gravy to taste and serve on the side of the roast.

MASTER RECIPE:

HERBED BUTTERFLY LAMB

A butterfly of lamb is a leg with the bone removed. This is a wonderful dish for the summer, as you can simply throw it on a hot grill. Or, you can prepare it indoors by broiling the meat until crisp and brown and then baking it with the marinade until tender.

The lamb is marinated for at least 24 hours, and preferably 48, in a savory herb-infused mixture. The marinade not only gives the lamb tremendous flavor, but also tenderizes it while it sits. Serve with roasted or boiled baby new potatoes (or a simple potato salad) and a red onion, tomato, and watercress salad.

SERVES 8.

The Marinade:
$2/3$ cup olive or vegetable oil
$1/2$ cup dry red wine
1 tablespoon balsamic or red wine vinegar
$1 1/2$ tablespoons Dijon mustard
$1/2$ cup chopped onions
3 cloves garlic, minced
1 tablespoon minced fresh ginger, or 1 teaspoon powdered
1 tablespoon chopped fresh basil, or 1 teaspoon crumbled dried
1 tablespoon chopped fresh mint, or 1 teaspoon crumbled dried
Generous grinding of black pepper
Salt (optional)

The Lamb:
1 leg of lamb, about 6 pounds*
Watercress and fresh mint sprigs for garnish

*Ask the butcher to remove the bone ("butterfly" the meat) and any excess fat. Keep the bone for making stock (page 90).

1. In a medium saucepan whisk together the oil, wine, vinegar, and mustard. Add all the remaining marinade ingredients and simmer over moderate heat for 10 minutes. Let cool.

2. Place the lamb in a large bowl and pour the marinade over it, making sure to coat the meat on all sides. Cover and refrigerate for at least 24 hours, turning the lamb at least once or twice.

3. Preheat the broiler or grill.

4. Remove the lamb, being sure to reserve the marinade. Place the meat in a large, shallow roasting pan and broil, fat side up, for 10 minutes. Turn lamb over and broil 10 minutes on the other side. Remove the meat and reduce the oven to 350 degrees. Pour the marinade over the lamb and roast about 20 to 25 minutes, or until it is slightly pink in the center. (To barbecue the lamb, remove the marinade and pour into a saucepan. Grill the meat over the hot coals about 15 minutes on each side, or until slightly pink in the center. Cook the marinade over moderate heat until slightly reduced, and pour over the cooked lamb.) Let meat sit about 5 minutes before carving. Serve with watercress and fresh mint springs.

MASTER RECIPE:

BRAISED SHOULDER OF LAMB

A shoulder of lamb is ideal for braising, as it results in a tender, succulent, fall-off-the-bone piece of meat and a rich vegetable and beef broth. The lamb can be served on its own, with the sauce on top, or you can add cooked white beans to the broth and serve the beans and broth alongside the lamb.

You'll get the best results with this dish if you prepare it a day before serving. That way the meat and broth can cool, and you can easily remove any excess fat. On the day you serve, all you have to do is heat up the lamb, strain the broth, and put it on the table. If you have lots of time you might want to use the bone from the shoulder of lamb to make stock. You can then use the homemade stock instead of beef broth for the sauce.

This recipe is an adaptation of Michael Field's Braised Shoulder of Lamb with White Beans, from his book *Culinary Classics & Improvisations* (Alfred A. Knopf, 1965).

SERVES 4.

About 1 cup flour seasoned with salt and pepper
1 (7½-pound) shoulder of lamb, boned and tied (about 4 to
   4½ pounds boned)
1½ tablespoons vegetable oil
1½ tablespoons olive oil
2½ cups thinly sliced leeks, about 1 large leek
2 cups thinly sliced carrots
2 cups thinly sliced celery
2 tablespoons minced garlic
1½ tablespoons minced fresh thyme, or 2 teaspoons crumbled dried
2 cups beef or lamb stock, preferably homemade (pages 18 and 90)
1 cup dry white wine
2 cups chopped ripe or canned tomatoes
Salt
Freshly ground black pepper
1 bay leaf
½ cup minced fresh parsley
3½ cups cooked white beans (page 253) or canned white beans,
   drained (optional)

1. Preheat the oven to 325 degrees.

2. Place the seasoned flour on a large plate, and lightly coat all sides of the lamb.

3. In a large ovenproof casserole, heat the vegetable oil over moderately high heat. Brown the lamb on all sides; remove and set aside.

4. Discard the oil and wipe out the casserole. Heat the olive oil in the casserole over moderate heat. Add the leeks, carrots, celery, garlic, and half the thyme and sauté about 10 minutes, or until soft but not brown. Add the lamb to the casserole, and pour in the stock, wine, tomatoes, salt, pepper, bay leaf, 1 tablespoon parsley, and the remaining thyme. Bring the liquids to a boil, and remove from the heat.

5. Cover the casserole and place in the preheated oven. Braise the lamb for about $2\frac{1}{2}$ to 3 hours, basting once or twice, until the meat is very soft when pierced with a fork.

6. Cool the meat in the broth, preferably overnight.

7. Using a large spoon, take off the layer of fat that's formed on top of the broth. Remove the meat from the broth.

8. Bring the broth to a simmer over moderate heat. Strain the broth into a large bowl, pressing down on the vegetables. Place the strained broth, and any of the vegetables that are still intact (particularly the carrot slices), back in the casserole. Add the lamb and optional cooked beans and simmer about 10 minutes.

9. Place the lamb on a serving platter and remove any string. Thinly slice the lamb and serve with the optional beans (and any remaining vegetables) on the side. Cover with the hot broth and sprinkle the remaining parsley on top.

LAMB STOCK

You would think that after roasting a leg of lamb for several hours the bone wouldn't be of much use for anything. In fact, the lamb bones are surprisingly full of flavor and they can be used to produce a delicate stock.

If there is quite a bit of meat clinging to the lamb bone be sure to remove it and save it for a soup or stew. But any little bits of meat can be left on the bone because they add good flavor to the stock.

MAKES ABOUT 8 CUPS.

Bone from a 6-pound leg of lamb, cut in half
3 stalks of celery, cut into small pieces
2 carrots, cut into small pieces
2 onions, peeled and quartered
1 large ripe tomato or 1 cup canned tomato, cut into small pieces
$1/2$ cup red wine
Any drippings from the roast lamb
4 peppercorns
1 bay leaf
Small sprig of fresh parsley
Pinch of salt

1. Put all the ingredients in a large soup pot or stockpot and add enough water just to cover the lamb bone. Bring to a boil over high heat, reduce the heat, and simmer, partially covered, for about 1 to 2 hours, or until the stock is somewhat reduced and flavorful. If it tastes weak, simply raise the heat a bit and let it reduce further.

2. Drain the stock into a colander set over a large bowl. Remove the bones and cut any remaining meat off and set aside. Discard the vegetables and bones. Remove any fat that has floated to the top. The stock can then be refrigerated or frozen, or used right away to make a soup.

Lamb, Lentil, and Rosemary Soup

The flavor of fresh rosemary is an essential part of this thick, meaty soup. Serve with a mixed green salad and top with garlicky croutons.

SERVES 4 TO 6.

2 tablespoons olive oil
1 tablespoon butter
3 garlic cloves, minced
2 onions, chopped
2 carrots, cut into small cubes
2 1/2 tablespoons chopped fresh rosemary, or 1 tablespoon crumbled dried
1 tablespoon chopped fresh thyme, or 1 teaspoon crumbled dried
Salt
Freshly ground black pepper
6 cups lamb stock (page 90)
2 cups chopped very ripe tomatoes or canned tomatoes
1 1/4 cups lentils, rinsed
1 bay leaf
1 bone from a roast leg of lamb
1 cup cubed cooked lamb
Tabasco or other liquid hot pepper sauce

1. In a large soup pot, heat the olive oil and butter over moderately low heat. Add the garlic, onions, carrots, half the rosemary, the thyme, and salt and pepper to taste. Simmer, covered, over low heat for 15 to 20 minutes, or until tender. Add the lamb stock, tomatoes, lentils, bay leaf, and the lamb bone from the roast if you still have it and bring the soup to a boil. Reduce the heat and simmer, partially covered, for about 40 minutes, or until the lentils are tender. Taste for seasoning.

2. To serve, place a small handful of cooked lamb in the bottom of each soup bowl and ladle the hot soup over it. Garnish with the remaining fresh rosemary. Serve with a bottle of Tabasco on the side.

Nancy's Lamb, Orzo, and Dill Soup

SERVES 6 TO 8.

1 bone from a leg of lamb, with bits of meat clinging to it
1 28-ounce can tomatoes, chopped, or 4 large, very ripe tomatoes,
    chopped
3 carrots, chopped
3 stalks celery, chopped
3 onions, chopped
10 peppercorns
Handful of chopped fresh parsley
Salt
1 cup orzo or small tubular pasta
1/2 cup fresh dill, chopped

1. In a large stockpot, combine the bone, tomatoes, carrots, celery, onions, peppercorns, parsley, and salt. Add 12 cups cold water and bring the soup to a boil. Reduce the heat, skim off any foam that rises to the top, and simmer, partially covered, for about 1 1/2 hours to 2 hours. Taste for seasoning. If the soup seems weak let it simmer with the lid off for an additional 30 minutes.

2. Just before serving the soup, bring a large pot of lightly salted water to a boil. Add the orzo and boil for about 10 minutes, or until just tender. Strain the orzo and add it to the soup along with the dill. Remove the lamb bone, scrape off any meat, and add it to the soup. Taste for seasoning and serve hot with a loaf of sourdough bread.

Lamb, Leek, and Potato Chowder

This chowder can be made using lamb, chicken, or beef stock. You can also add some finely chopped leftover cooked spinach, kale, asparagus, or a few lettuce leaves. Serve with a tossed salad, warm bread, and a good bottle of dry red wine.

SERVES ABOUT 4.

1 tablespoon olive oil
1 tablespoon butter
4 cups thinly sliced leeks (about 1 large or 2 medium), white and
    light green parts
3 cups peeled cubed potatoes
1 1/2 teaspoons chopped fresh rosemary, or 3/4 teaspoon crumbled
    dried
1 cup dry red wine
7 cups lamb stock (page 90)
About 1 cup thinly sliced cooked lamb
1 to 2 cups cooked spinach, asparagus, lettuce, kale, or other
    flavorful green, chopped into small pieces (optional)
Salt
Freshly ground black pepper
Sprigs of fresh rosemary
Freshly grated Parmesan cheese (optional)

1. In a large soup pot heat the oil and butter over moderately low heat. Add the leeks, cover, and cook about 5 minutes, stirring every few minutes to prevent burning.

2. Add the potatoes and rosemary and cook for about a minute. Raise the heat to high and add the wine. Boil for about 2 minutes, reduce to moderate heat, and add the stock. Simmer, partially covered, for about 1 hour, or until the stock is somewhat reduced and full of flavor and the potatoes are tender. Add the pieces of lamb, and any cooked green vegetable; simmer another 2 to 3 minutes. Season to taste. Garnish each bowl of soup with a sprig of fresh rosemary and pass the grated cheese in a small bowl on the side.

■■
Lamb and Barley Soup

This is a thick soup, perfect for a cold winter's day. You can save any remaining meat from the lamb bone and add just a bit to the soup before serving to make it even heartier.

SERVES 5–6.

> **About 7 cups lamb stock (page 90)**
> **1½ tablespoons chopped fresh basil, or 1 teaspoon crumbled dried basil**
> **1½ tablespoons chopped fresh thyme, or 1 teaspoon crumbled dried thyme**
> **⅔ cup quick-cooking pearl barley**
> **2 tablespoons chopped fresh dill**

1. Bring the stock to a boil in a large pot. Reduce the heat and simmer about 1 hour with the basil and thyme, until slightly thickened. Add the barley and half the dill and simmer 10 to 15 minutes, or until the barley is soft and the soup is thickened. (If the soup is too thick, thin it with water.)

2. Add any chopped lamb meat and warm through. Sprinkle with the remaining tablespoon of fresh dill and serve.

Chinese Lamb Hot Pot

This deceptively simple stew takes only minutes to put together, but it is full of interesting and exotic flavors and textures. Serve with a large bowl of white rice and a steamed leafy green vegetable such as spinach or bok choy.

SERVES 2.

> **6 dried Chinese mushrooms**
> **1 tablespoon safflower oil**
> **3 garlic cloves, minced**
> **1 shallot, chopped**
> **2 scallions, chopped, green and white parts kept separate**
> **2 cups 1-inch cubes cooked leg of lamb, butterfly, or shoulder**
> **1 cup lamb or chicken stock (pages 90, 193)**
> **2 tablespoons coarsely chopped fresh ginger**
> **12 peeled fresh water chestnuts, or 1 cup canned, cut in half**
> **1 tablespoon soy sauce**
> **3 tablespoons Chinese oyster sauce**
> **1/2 to 1 teaspoon Chinese chile paste, depending on the degree of spiciness you want**
> **1 teaspoon cornstarch**
> **1/3 cup chopped fresh coriander**
> **Sesame oil**

1. Place the dried mushrooms in a small bowl and cover with boiling water. Let soak for about 30 minutes, or until soft. Drain, pat dry, and cut into thick slices.

2. In a large, heavy casserole, heat the oil over moderate heat. Sauté the garlic, shallot, and the white part of the scallions for about 1 minute. Add the lamb and sauté for a few seconds. Add the stock, ginger, water chestnuts, reserved mushrooms, soy sauce, oyster sauce, and chile paste. Simmer, covered, over moderate heat for about 4 minutes.

3. Put the cornstarch in a small bowl and stir in a few tablespoons of the broth from the stew. Slowly add the cornstarch paste to the stew and simmer a minute, or until slightly thickened.

4. Drizzle a tiny amount of sesame oil over each bowl of stew and serve with the scallion greens and coriander in small bowls on the side.

LAMB SANDWICH IDEAS

➤LAMB, FETA, AND TOMATO
Thinly sliced lamb on thickly sliced homemade white bread layered with feta cheese, tomatoes, lettuce, mayonnaise, and black pepper.

➤LAMB CHAPATI
Chapati is the Indian version of a whole wheat tortilla, available in health and specialty food stores. Heat the chapati in a warm oven. Spread with yogurt, thin slices of lamb, chopped fresh mint leaves, thinly sliced cucumber, and shredded lettuce. Roll into a fat cigar shape.

➤MOROCCAN-STYLE SANDWICH
Take a warm pita bread or a lightly toasted slice of peasant-style bread and spread very lightly with Moroccan Hot Sauce (page 236). Top with slices of lamb, thinly sliced pitted black olives, and paper-thin slices of red onion.

➤LAMB, CHUTNEY, AND CHEESE
An adaptation of a traditional English sandwich: Spread mango chutney on 2 very thin slices of brown bread with the crusts removed. Top with bite-sized pieces of lamb and thin slices of cheddar cheese. You could also use thin slivers of cucumber instead of cheese. Serve with a pot of Earl Grey tea.

Lamb Curry

Curry is a time-honored way of using leftover lamb. Serve over white rice and serve with cold beer or a crisp white wine and lots of condiments—chutney, grated coconut, raisins, chopped nuts.

SERVES 2 TO 3.

1 tablespoon butter
1 tablespoon safflower or vegetable oil
2 medium onions, thinly sliced
1 garlic clove, minced
2 tablespoons flour
1 1/2 to 2 teaspoons curry powder
1/2 teaspoon ground cumin
2 cups chicken stock (page 193)
2 cups bite-sized pieces cooked leg or butterfly of lamb, or braised
  lamb
1/2 cup raisins
2 tablespoons chopped crystallized ginger, or 1 tablespoon minced
  fresh ginger
Dash of Tabasco or other liquid hot pepper sauce
1 1/2 tablespoons heavy cream

1. In a large skillet, heat the butter and oil over moderate heat. Sauté the onions and garlic until soft, about 5 minutes. Add the flour, the curry powder, and 1/4 teaspoon of the cumin and stir well. Let cook for several seconds. Whisk in the chicken stock and raise the heat to high. Bring the mixture to a boil, reduce the heat, and simmer for 5 minutes, or until thickened. Add the lamb, raisins, and ginger and simmer another 5 minutes.

2. Just before serving, add the hot pepper sauce, and remaining cumin to taste. Stir in the cream and heat for 1 minute.

3. Serve with bowls of grated coconut, raisins, mango chutney, chopped almonds, and chopped crystallized ginger.

Middle Eastern Lamb Sandwiches

This is a wonderful sandwich for a hot summer lunch or a light supper. Fresh mint is essential to the flavor of the sauce. This recipe makes 3 sandwiches; if you have enough leftover lamb, it can easily be doubled or tripled.

Serve with a thinly sliced cucumber and mint salad and a chilled dry white wine.

SERVES 3.

The Sauce:

2/3 cup yogurt
2/3 cup tahini
1 small onion, finely chopped
2 tablespoons finely chopped fresh mint
1 tablespoon finely chopped fresh parsley
1 1/2 tablespoons fresh lime juice
1/2 teaspoon Tabasco or other liquid hot pepper sauce
1/2 teaspoon olive oil
Pinch of sugar
Pinch of salt

The Meat and Sandwich:

3 8-inch pita pockets
1 1/2 tablespoons olive oil
1 small onion, finely chopped
1 garlic clove, finely chopped
1 teaspoon ground cumin
12 thin slices cooked leg of lamb (3 to 4 cups)
Pinch of salt
Generous grinding of black pepper
4 large lettuce leaves, shredded
1 ripe tomato, finely chopped

1. Prepare the sauce: Combine all the ingredients in a bowl. Taste for seasoning and add more hot pepper sauce, sugar, or salt, as needed. Set aside.

2. Prepare the sandwiches: Cut off about an inch at one end of the pita bread and warm in a low oven.

3. In a large skillet, heat the oil over moderate heat. Sauté the onion

and garlic for about 3 to 4 minutes, or until the onion is translucent. Stir in the cumin and cook for several seconds. Add the meat and cook about 1 minute on each side, or until warm. Season with salt and pepper.

4. Remove the pita pockets from the oven. Stuff the lettuce and tomatoes into the bottoms of the pockets. Add the meat and top with the sauce.

■■■

Open-Faced Lamb Sandwiches with Horseradish

The success of this sandwich depends on the quality and quantity of left-over gravy you have from your roast leg of lamb (page 85).

SERVES 1 OR 2.

> ¹/₂ loaf French or Italian bread, about an 8-inch piece of bread, or 2
>   pita breads
> 1 tablespoon olive or vegetable oil
> 1 medium onion, thinly sliced
> 1 cup thinly sliced cooked leg of lamb
> 3 to 4 tablespoons leftover gravy
> Small bowl of grated white horseradish, fresh or bottled, drained

1. Slice the bread into two 4-inch pieces. (If using pita bread, leave whole.) Place in warm oven and heat.

2. In a medium skillet, heat the oil over moderate heat. Sauté the onion for about 4 minutes, until golden brown but not burnt. Add the lamb and sauté a few seconds, then add the leftover gravy. Simmer about 3 minutes.

3. Remove the bread from the oven and slice the pieces down the middle lengthwise. Pour the warm lamb slices on top and drizzle liberally with the gravy. Place a small dollop of horseradish on top of each sandwich or serve the horseradish on the side.

Shepherdess Pie

This dish is quite a bit like shepherd's pie—the classic British dish of cooked meat and vegetables topped with a crown of mashed potatoes. My version is a bit spicier, more Mediterranean, somehow more feminine—thus its name. You can make this dish with or without mashed potatoes. If you decide to make them with, you'll need about 2 cups.

SERVES 2 TO 4.

> 2 tablespoons olive oil
> 3 garlic cloves, minced
> 2 large onions, thinly sliced
> 1 large green bell pepper, seeds and ribs removed, cut into small chunks
> 2 large ripe tomatoes, cut into small chunks, or 2 cups canned tomatoes
> 1/2 to 1 chile pepper, very thinly sliced into rings; do not remove the seeds*
> 1 tablespoon chopped fresh thyme, or 1 teaspoon crumbled dried
> 1/2 cup dry white wine
> Salt
> Freshly ground black pepper
> 1 19-ounce can cannellini (white kidney) beans, drained, or 1 1/2 cups fresh cooked beans (page 253)
> 1 1/2 cups cubed cooked lamb
> Any drippings from the roast lamb
> About 2 cups mashed potatoes (page 134)
> 1/4 cup bread crumbs (page 46)
> 1/4 cup freshly grated Parmesan cheese
> 1 1/2 tablespoons butter, cut into small bits
> Paprika

1. Preheat the oven to 400 degrees.
2. In a large ovenproof skillet or shallow casserole, heat the olive oil over moderately low heat. Sauté the garlic and onions, covered, for about 5 to 8 minutes, until soft and lightly golden but not brown. Add

---

*If you like very spicy food, add the whole chile; if not, add half or less.

the green pepper, tomatoes, chile pepper, thyme, wine, and salt and pepper to taste. Simmer, uncovered, for about 5 to 10 minutes, or until the tomatoes break down and have formed a sauce.

3. Add the drained beans, the lamb, and drippings. Simmer a minute and remove from the heat. You can serve the dish at this point and forget the potatoes; believe me, it will be delicious.

4. Using a large spoon or a piping bag, spread the mashed potatoes around the outside rim of the skillet or casserole. Sprinkle the bread crumbs on the potatoes, then the cheese, and dot with the butter. Sprinkle lightly with the paprika. (The entire dish can be made ahead up to this point and kept in the refrigerator for several hours before baking.)

5. Bake 15 minutes, or until the pie is hot and bubbling and the potatoes have a very light golden glaze.

■ ■

Lamejun
(Middle Eastern-Style Lamb Pizza)

Lamejun is traditionally made with a thin crust similar to Syrian bread and topped with finely ground lamb and/or beef, tomatoes, peppers, onions, parsley, and spices. Here is my variation.

This recipe makes enough dough for two 10-inch pizzas or 3 to 4 small pizzas. Any remaining dough can be frozen. I've given the measurements for enough lamb topping for one 10-inch pizza; the topping can easily be doubled or tripled.

There is another, simpler way to prepare Lamejun. Prepare the topping and spread on top of a pita bread split in half lengthwise, as described in step 9.

SERVES 2 TO 4.

The Dough:
1 tablespoon active dry yeast (1 envelope)
1½ cups *warm* water
About 3 to 3½ cups unbleached flour
½ teaspoon salt
2 tablespoons olive oil
Freshly ground black pepper
About 2 tablespoons cornmeal

(continued)

The Topping:

- 3 tablespoons olive oil
- 3 medium onions, very thinly sliced
- 10 sun-dried tomatoes (optional)
- 1 cup chopped cooked lamb
- 2 garlic cloves, chopped
- 2 ripe tomatoes or canned plum tomatoes
- 2 tablespoons chopped fresh parsley
- Pinch of salt
- 1/4 to 1/2 teaspoon Tabasco or other liquid hot pepper sauce
- 2 garlic cloves, very thinly sliced
- 1 1/2 tablespoons chopped fresh rosemary, or 1/2 tablespoon crumbled dried
- 1 1/2 tablespoons chopped fresh basil, or 1/2 tablespoon crumbled dried
- 1 1/2 tablespoons chopped fresh thyme, or 1/2 tablespoon crumbled dried
- 1/2 cup grated mozzarella or cheddar cheese
- 1/2 cup grated Parmesan or Romano cheese

1. Make the pizza dough: Mix the yeast with the water in a large bowl, and place in a warm spot for 5 minutes, or until the yeast begins to bubble and foam. (If the yeast does not foam, discard and begin again using fresh yeast.)

2. Sift 3 cups of the flour and the salt into the yeast mixture and gradually mix to form a ball. Mix in the olive oil, black pepper, and enough additional flour to form a soft ball.

3. Transfer the dough to a lightly floured work surface and knead until soft and elastic, about 10 minutes. Shape into a ball and place in a lightly oiled bowl; turn the dough over to coat with the oil on all sides. Cover with a clean tea towel and place in a warm, draft-free spot for about 1 hour, or until the dough has doubled in bulk.

4. Punch down the dough and reshape into a ball. Cover and let sit another 20 minutes, or until the dough rises again. Punch down and divide the dough in half or quarters, depending on the size of the pizza you're making. (To freeze any remaining dough, simply wrap in plastic; let thaw before proceeding.) Set the dough in the refrigerator until the topping is ready.

5. Make the topping: Heat 2 tablespoons of the olive oil in a large skillet over low heat. Sauté the onions for about 20 minutes, or until they are soft and a very light golden color. Remove from the heat.

6. If using dry (meaning unmarinated) sun-dried tomatoes, soak them in a bowl of hot water for 15 minutes, until softened. Drain and dry thoroughly on paper towels and slice into thin julienne strips. If using tomatoes marinated in olive oil, drain and slice into thin julienne strips.

7. In a chopping bowl or the bowl of a food processor, mix the lamb, chopped garlic, tomatoes, parsley, salt, and Tabasco. Chop or pulse until the mixture has the consistency of chopped meat. Set aside.

8. Preheat the oven to 500 degrees.

9. Working on a lightly floured surface, roll out half the dough into a 10-inch round. Sprinkle a baking sheet (or a pizza stone or ovenproof unglazed tiles) with the cornmeal and transfer the dough to it. Brush the top of the dough with the remaining tablespoon of olive oil. Sprinkle the dough with the garlic slices and herbs. Spread the onions on top in an even layer. Top with the lamb mixture and sun-dried tomatoes.

10. Bake the pizza for 3 to 4 minutes. Remove from the oven and sprinkle with the cheeses. Bake another 3 to 4 minutes, or until the cheese is bubbling and the crust is beginning to turn a golden brown.

Moussaka

This popular Greek dish can be made ahead and frozen or refrigerated until ready to bake.

SERVES 3 TO 4.

The Eggplant:
2 large eggplants
Salt
Vegetable oil

The White Sauce:
2¹/₂ tablespoons butter
2¹/₂ tablespoons flour
2¹/₂ cups milk
Grinding of fresh nutmeg
¹/₈ teaspoon ground cinnamon
3 tablespoons freshly grated Parmesan cheese

The Lamb Sauce:
1 tablespoon olive oil
1 large onion, chopped
4 cups ground cooked lamb*
2 cups canned or homemade tomato sauce (page 239)
¹/₄ cup chopped fresh parsley
¹/₈ teaspoon ground cinnamon
Freshly ground black pepper
Salt
¹/₂ cup freshly grated Parmesan cheese
1 tablespoon butter, cut into small pieces

1. Prepare the eggplants: Peel and cut into ¹/₂-inch-thick slices. Sprinkle generously with salt and place in a colander to drain. (This process, which the French call *dégorgement*, removes any excess liquid and bitterness from the eggplant.) Let sit for 30 minutes. Rinse and dry thoroughly on paper towels.

2. Heat a large skillet over high heat. Coat the bottom with oil and

---

*To grind the lamb: Place pieces of chopped lamb in a food processor and process, bit by bit, until the lamb is ground but not too fine. This can also be done in a chopping bowl.

brown the eggplant on both sides, about 30 seconds to a side. If the eggplant soaks up all the oil (which it's very prone to do), simply add more or let the heat brown the eggplant without adding more oil. Drain on paper towels to remove any excess grease.

3. Meanwhile, make the white sauce: In a medium saucepan, melt the butter over moderate heat. Add the flour and stir together to form a roux. Let cook for a few seconds, until the roux turns a light golden color. Slowly whisk in the milk and let the sauce come to a boil. Reduce the heat, stir in the nutmeg and cinnamon, and simmer over very low heat until thickened. Stir in the cheese.

4. Preheat the oven to 350 degrees.

5. Prepare the lamb: In a medium skillet, heat the olive oil over moderate heat. Sauté the onion for 4 or 5 minutes, add the ground lamb, and brown for about 30 seconds. Add the tomato sauce and parsley, cinnamon, pepper, and salt and let simmer about 5 minutes, until heated through. Set aside.

6. Very lightly oil the bottom of a shallow 6- to 8-cup casserole or medium baking pan. Line with half the eggplant. Top with the lamb mixture and then another layer of eggplant. Pour the white sauce on top and sprinkle with the cheese and butter. (The dish can be made ahead up to this point. It can be frozen or kept in the refrigerator for several days before baking. Thaw or bring to room temperature before baking.)

7. Bake for about 20 minutes, or until golden brown and bubbling.

Spinach Linguine with Lamb, Leeks, and Roasted Red Peppers

SERVES 2 TO 4.

1 large red bell pepper
1 large leek or 2 small ones
3 tablespoons olive oil
3 garlic cloves, minced
$^1/_2$ to $^3/_4$ cup cubed cooked lamb, ham, pork, sausage, or duck
3 tablespoons chopped sun-dried tomatoes
3 tablespoons drained capers
1 tablespoon chopped fresh rosemary, or 1 teaspoon crumbled dried
Freshly ground black pepper
$^1/_2$ cup dry white wine
$^1/_2$ pound spinach linguine, preferably fresh
Freshly grated Parmesan cheese

1. Preheat the broiler. Set a large pot of lightly salted water on to boil.

2. Place the pepper on a piece of aluminum foil and broil about 3 minutes on each side, until the pepper is completely charred. Remove from the broiler and wrap pepper in foil about 3 minutes. Take off the foil and with a small, sharp knife peel the charred skin off the pepper. Cut in half, remove the seeds and core, cut in thick slices, and set aside.

3. Cut the top few inches of green off the leek and discard. Cut the leek in quarters lengthwise and rinse thoroughly. Cut into 2- to 3-inch pieces.

4. In a medium skillet, heat the olive oil over moderately low heat. Add the leeks and garlic and sauté gently for about 20 minutes, or until the leeks have softened. Add the reserved peppers, lamb, sun-dried tomatoes, capers, rosemary, and pepper; sauté for about 30 seconds. Raise the heat, add the wine, and let simmer until the wine is reduced by about half. Keep warm over very low heat until the pasta is ready.

5. Meanwhile, add the spinach linguine to the boiling water. Cook just a few minutes if fresh and about 8 to 10 minutes if dried, or until al dente. Drain and toss with the lamb sauce. Serve grated Parmesan cheese on the side.

Stir-Fried Lamb with Favas and Red Peppers

Los Angeles-based food consultant, spokesperson, and writer Jan Weimer says she'll do just about anything to avoid going to the supermarket at the end of a long workday. This simple stir-fry was put together one night when she had some leftover lamb and assorted vegetables in the refrigerator. Serve it over a plate of steamed rice.

You can substitute 1 pound of cooked asparagus, beans, or any other vegetable for the fava beans.

SERVES 2 TO 3.

1 pound fresh fava beans, shells and outer skins removed
3 tablespoons olive oil
3 large garlic cloves, minced
3 scallions, white part only, thinly sliced
2 red bell peppers, seeded and cut into ¼-inch julienne strips
1 small zucchini, cut into ¼-inch julienne strips
1½ to 2 cups cooked lamb, cut into ¼-inch julienne strips, at room temperature
2 small tomatoes, peeled, seeded, and cut into ¼-inch dice
1½ tablespoons minced fresh herbs (savory, thyme, oregano, parsley, etc.)
Salt
Freshly ground black pepper

1. In a medium saucepan, bring 1 cup of water to a boil. Add the favas and cook about 3 minutes, or until easily pierced with a knife. Drain and set aside.

2. Heat the olive oil in a wok or large skillet over moderately high heat. Add the garlic and scallions and stir-fry for about 1 minute. Add the red peppers and cook an additional minute. Add the zucchini and the reserved favas and stir-fry another minute. Add the lamb, tomatoes, and herbs and cook 1 minute, or until heated through. Season with salt and pepper. Serve over rice.

Lamb with Tomatoes, Olives, and Lemon Zest

This is a quick, easy sauté you can put together in minutes. Serve topped with a dollop of sour cream and thinly sliced raw scallions.

SERVES 2.

> 1 tablespoon olive oil
> 1 tablespoon butter
> 3 scallions, cut into 2-inch pieces
> 1 cup thinly sliced cooked leg of lamb, preferably pink, butterfly of
>   lamb, or shoulder
> 1 large ripe tomato, cubed
> 1 tablespoon grated lemon zest
> 1 cup black olives, preferably Calamata, pitted and left whole or cut
>   in half
> Salt
> Freshly ground black pepper
> About ½ cup sour cream
> 1 scallion, thinly sliced

1. In a medium skillet, heat the oil and butter over moderate heat. Sauté the scallions for about 1 minute, until slightly softened but not brown.

2. Add the lamb, stir for a few seconds, toss in the tomato, and sauté another 2 minutes, stirring frequently. Gently stir in the lemon zest and olives and salt and pepper and heat through. Serve immediately with the sour cream and scallions on the side.

Lamb-and-Rice-Stuffed Zucchini

These delicately flavored stuffed zucchini make a great first course or a main course, accompanied by a large mixed salad, grilled tomatoes, and a warm loaf of French bread.

There are several variations of this recipe that work well: use cooked orzo instead of rice, and substitute beef for the lamb. You can also substitute cooked shrimp for the lamb, and add a touch of lemon juice, a few chopped almonds, and fresh thyme instead of the cinnamon.

SERVES 2.

2 medium-small zucchini
2¹/₂ tablespoons olive oil
3 garlic cloves, chopped
1 cup ground or very finely chopped cooked lamb or beef
1 cup cooked rice or orzo
Salt
Freshly ground black pepper
¹/₃ cup minced fresh parsley
1 teaspoon ground cinnamon
¹/₃ cup tomato sauce, bottled or homemade (page 239)
¹/₃ cup bread crumbs (page 46)

1. Preheat the oven to 400 degrees.

2. Cut the stem end off the zucchini, and cut down the center lengthwise. Using a melon scooper or a small spoon, carefully remove the flesh of the zucchini, making sure to leave the skin intact. Chop the flesh fine and set aside. Place the zucchini shells in a lightly oiled shallow baking dish and brush the inside of each shell with a touch of olive oil (about ¹/₂ tablespoon total).

3. In a medium skillet, heat 1 tablespoon of the oil over moderate heat. Sauté the garlic and chopped zucchini for about 2 minutes. Add the lamb, rice, salt, pepper, parsley, and cinnamon; sauté 1 minute. Add the tomato sauce, stir thoroughly, and remove from the heat.

4. Spoon the filling into the zucchini shells, mounding the stuffing slightly. Sprinkle the bread crumbs on top and drizzle with the remaining olive oil (The recipe can be made ahead up to this point and covered and refrigerated for several hours until ready to bake.)

5. Add enough water to the pan to come about one third of the way up the zucchini. Bake for about 20 minutes, or until the zucchini feels tender when gently prodded with a fork. Place under the broiler for a minute or two until the topping is golden brown.

Mushrooms Stuffed with Lamb, Parsley, and Pine Nuts

These hors d'oeuvres can be prepared several hours before serving and refrigerated until ready to bake.

SERVES 3 TO 6.

About 5 to 6 slices cooked lamb
4 tablespoons freshly grated Parmesan cheese
4 tablespoons bread crumbs (page 46)
1 tablespoon chopped fresh rosemary, or 1 1/2 teaspoons crumbled
dried
4 tablespoons chopped fresh parsley
1/2 tablespoon butter
1/2 tablespoon olive oil
1/2 cup finely chopped onions
12 medium mushrooms
1/4 cup pine nuts
1/4 cup heavy cream
1 tablespoon butter, cut into 12 small pieces

1. Grind the lamb in a food processor or blender; set aside. (You can also finely chop the lamb using a sharp knife.)
2. In a small bowl, combine the cheese, bread crumbs, half the rosemary, and 1 tablespoon of the parsley; set aside.
3. In a medium skillet, heat the butter and olive oil over moderately low heat. Sauté the onions and the remaining rosemary for about 8 minutes, or until soft but not brown.
4. Preheat the oven to 350 degrees.
5. Meanwhile, remove the stems from the mushrooms and set aside. Very lightly grease a baking pan or ovenproof skillet with olive oil. Place the whole mushroom caps in the pan or skillet.
6. Put the mushroom stems and the remaining parsley in a food processor or blender and blend until coarsely ground. Add the pine nuts and process for just a few seconds, until the nuts are coarsely chopped but not pureed.
7. Add the ground lamb and the mushroom/nut mixture to the skillet and sauté 1 minute. Pour in the cream and sauté another minute. Remove from the heat and stir in 2 tablespoons of the cheese/bread crumb mixture and the sautéed onions.

8. Spoon the mixture into the mushroom caps, pressing down lightly to get as much filling in each cap as possible. (The recipe can be made ahead up to this point, covered, and refrigerated for several hours until ready to bake.)

9. Sprinkle the remaining cheese/bread crumb mixture over the tops of the mushrooms and dot each one with a small piece of butter.

10. Bake for 15 minutes, until the mushrooms have softened and the stuffing is very hot. Serve immediately.

SEE ALSO:

5

PASTA, RICE, and POTATOES

PASTA, RICE, AND POTATOES: RECIPE LISTING

PASTA

MASTER RECIPES: RICE

LEFTOVER RECIPES: RICE

MASTER RECIPES: POTATOES

LEFTOVER RECIPES: POTATOES

A WORD ABOUT PASTA

➤Virtually any type of cooked pasta can be used in these leftover recipes. The one exception, however, is pasta that is overcooked and gummy—toss it.

➤If you are working with pasta that is sauced—be it butter and cheese, tomato, seafood, or meat—and you think the sauce will conflict with the flavor of the leftover recipe, remove it before proceeding. You can either rinse the pasta under very hot water and gently pat it dry with paper towels or simply blot it off with paper towels.

██

Gratin of Pasta with Herb Cheese Sauce

This is an extremely quick, easy way to make leftover pasta taste (dare I say) even better than it was the day before.

I first tried this recipe using leftover spaghetti and meatballs in a tomato sauce. Then I tried it again using linguine with a garlic, herb, and shrimp sauce and it worked just as well. The point is that you can use virtually any type of leftover pasta with this recipe. Add bits of cooked ham or sausage, slices of cooked vegetables, even bits of leftover seafood or poultry.

SERVES 2.

2 tablespoons butter
1 tablespoon flour
1 cup milk
2 tablespoons chopped fresh basil, or 1 tablespoon crumbled dried
$1/3$ cup chopped fresh parsley
Salt
Freshly ground black pepper
$1/2$ cup freshly grated Parmesan cheese
2 cups cooked pasta
Meatballs, sausage, ham, chicken or seafood, cut into small pieces

1. Preheat the oven to 400 degrees.
2. To make the sauce, melt 1 tablespoon of the butter in a medium saucepan over moderate heat. Add the flour and stir well to create a roux. Gradually add the milk, whisking until smooth, and let the sauce come to a boil. Reduce the heat and let simmer until it thickens. Add the basil, 2 tablespoons of the parsley, and salt and pepper to taste. Slowly stir in three quarters of the grated cheese. Taste for seasoning.
3. Grease the bottom of a medium casserole (with a lid) with the remaining tablespoon of butter. Add the pasta and top with sliced meat, poultry, or fish if desired. Pour the sauce over the pasta, making sure it coats all the pasta as well as the bottom of the casserole. Top with the remaining cheese, cover, and bake for 10 minutes. Remove the lid and let the cheese brown for 5 minutes. Top with the remaining parsley.

Pasta Shells with Asparagus, Feta Cheese, Tomato, and Dill

You can add any type of cooked vegetable you'd like to this salad—chopped spinach or kale, peas, red and green pepper, artichoke hearts, or bits of broccoli.

SERVES 2 TO 4.

$^1/_2$ **pound cooked pasta shells**
$^1/_2$ **pound cooked asparagus, cut into small pieces**
$^3/_4$ **cup feta cheese, cut into small cubes**
1 cup cherry tomatoes, cut in half
$^1/_4$ **cup chopped fresh dill**
1$^1/_2$ tablespoons minced fresh parsley
2$^1/_2$ tablespoons olive oil
1 tablespoon red wine vinegar
Juice of $^1/_2$ lemon
Salt
Freshly ground black pepper
Dill flowers for garnish (optional)

1. Put the pasta in a serving bowl and toss with the cooked asparagus, feta, tomatoes, dill, parsley, olive oil, vinegar, and lemon juice. Add salt and pepper to taste.
2. Garnish with dill flowers and serve at room temperature.

■ ■

Pasta Frittata

This surprisingly good concoction is great for a Sunday morning, particularly if you have some leftover pasta from a weekend meal. Any type of leftover pasta will work well in this recipe. You can also add bits of ham or prosciutto, chopped cooked spinach, raw mushrooms, or other vegetables.

SERVES 4.

1¹/₂ tablespoons butter
1 teaspoon olive oil
1 small onion, chopped
1 clove garlic, chopped
1 tablespoon chopped fresh basil, or ¹/₂ teaspoon crumbled dried
1¹/₂ tablespoons chopped fresh tarragon, or ³/₄ teaspoon crumbled dried
4 large eggs
1 tablespoon heavy cream
2 tablespoons tomato sauce, bottled or homemade (page 239), or
    1 small ripe tomato, finely chopped*
Salt
Freshly ground black pepper
2 cups cooked pasta
¹/₄ cup plus 1 tablespoon freshly grated Parmesan cheese

1. Preheat the oven to 400 degrees.
2. In a medium ovenproof skillet, heat 1 tablespoon of the butter and the oil over moderate heat. Add the onion, garlic, and half the basil and tarragon and sauté 8 minutes, or until soft but not brown.
3. Meanwhile, in a medium bowl, whisk the eggs, cream, the remaining basil and tarragon, tomato sauce, salt, and pepper.
4. Add the pasta to the onion mixture along with the remaining ¹/₂ tablespoon of butter and stir thoroughly. Raise the heat to high, pour the egg mixture over the pasta, stirring gently just to mix the eggs with the pasta, and cook about 30 seconds, or until the mixture around the edge of the skillet starts to bubble.
5. Bake the frittata 15 minutes, or until slightly puffed. Sprinkle with the cheese and bake another 2 to 4 minutes, or until golden brown.

*If the leftover pasta is already in a tomato sauce, omit the tomato.

Macaroni in a Bacon, Basil Cream Sauce

You can use any type of leftover cooked shaped pasta with this recipe.

SERVES 2.

2 strips bacon
2 cups cooked shaped pasta
¹/₄ cup heavy cream
¹/₄ cup chicken stock (page 193)
1¹/₂ tablespoons chopped fresh basil, or 1 teaspoon crumbled dried
Freshly ground black pepper
Freshly grated Parmesan cheese

1. In a medium skillet, fry the bacon until just crisp. Drain on paper towels and set aside. Remove all but 1 teaspoon of the bacon fat from the pan.

2. Place the skillet over moderate heat and add the pasta. Stir well to coat. Add the cream, stock, and basil and simmer about 8 minutes, or until the sauce is reduced and slightly thickened. Season with pepper and serve with the grated cheese on the side.

■■■
Grady's Spaghetti Omelette

"Frying spaghetti," says my friend, writer John Grady, "is an art unto itself." This omelette can be served whole and puffed up soufflé-style, or folded into a more traditional omelette.

SERVES 2 TO 4.

> 2 tablespoons butter
> 2 cups cooked spaghetti or other pasta
> 1 small clove garlic, chopped (optional)
> 1 cup chopped or sliced assorted vegetables (onions, bell peppers, mushrooms, etc.)
> 4 large eggs
> 1/2 cup milk
> Salt
> Freshly ground black pepper
> Pinch fresh or dried herbs (basil, oregano, thyme, etc.)
> 1 cup assorted grated cheeses

1. In a large skillet, melt the butter over moderately low heat. Add the cooked spaghetti and cook about 5 minutes, or until it begins to get crispy and golden. Add the garlic and vegetables and continue to cook, stirring frequently, for another 5 minutes, or until the vegetables are soft and the pasta has begun to turn golden brown.

2. Whisk the eggs with the milk, salt, pepper, and herbs. If you're going to be leaving the omelette whole (and not folding it), whisk the cheese into the egg mixture.

3. Pour the egg mixture over the pasta and let it spread out over all the pasta. If you're leaving the omelette whole, let it cook about 2 minutes, or until the eggs start to set. Then flip it like a pancake. Cook another 2 or 3 minutes on the other side, or until the eggs have set. If you want to fold the omelette, sprinkle the cheeses on top and let cook about 2 to 3 minutes, or until the eggs start to cook. Flip the omelette in half and cook another 2 to 3 minutes, or until the eggs have set.

■■

Ken Hom's Pasta Stir-Fry

This recipe was adapted from one given to me by a favorite cook of mine, Ken Hom. Through his cookbooks, television cooking shows, and cooking classes, Hom has built a reputation for combining Eastern and Western ingredients and techniques. This dish combines Western ingredients (cooked pasta, olive oil, peppers, sun-dried tomatoes, herbs, and bits of leftover meat) with an Oriental method of cooking—stir-frying.

You can use just about any shape of pasta in this dish, though Hom favors fusilli. I tried the dish with some chopped cooked ham but you can easily substitute beef, lamb, pork, or poultry. You can also add leftover chopped vegetables and leave out the meat altogether.

SERVES 2 TO 4.

1 tablespoon olive oil
2 garlic cloves, chopped
2 small shallots, chopped
1 small onion, chopped
1 green bell pepper, seeded and chopped
1/3 cup chopped fresh basil
1 cup cubed cooked ham (or beef, lamb, pork, chicken, or turkey)
1/3 cup finely chopped sun-dried tomatoes (drained if marinated)
3/4 tablespoon tomato paste
1/2 pound cooked pasta (about 4 cups)
Salt
Freshly ground black pepper
2 scallions, chopped
Freshly grated Parmesan cheese

1. Heat the oil in a wok or large skillet over moderately high heat. Add half the garlic, the shallots, and onion and cook about 2 minutes. Add the pepper, half the basil, the ham, sun-dried tomatoes, and tomato paste and stir-fry another 2 minutes.

2. Add the cooked pasta, the remaining garlic and basil, and about 1/3 cup water and stir thoroughly. Cook, stirring constantly, until the water thickens a bit and forms a tomatoey sauce, about 3 to 4 minutes. Season with salt and pepper. Serve with the scallions scattered over the top and the grated cheese on the side.

MASTER RECIPE:

RICE

I am always amazed to meet experienced cooks who claim they can't make a good pot of rice. The key to good rice is slow cooking and good-quality rice.

My favorite is brown rice. Brown rice is what rice looks like after the inedible husk is removed. It has a light brown color that comes from the natural bran layers left on the grain. Brown rice has a slightly chewy texture and nutty, grainy flavor. It takes longer to cook than white rice—about 40 to 50 minutes.

Once the bran layer is removed from brown rice it is called white rice. There are several sizes of white rice—long, medium, and short grain. Long- and medium-grain rice are ideal for curries and paella and for serving with meat, poultry, fish, and vegetable dishes. Short-grain rice is a bit moister and stickier, making it the perfect choice for puddings, cakes, and sushi. White rice generally takes about 15 minutes to cook.

Precooked or "quick" rice is also available. This is white rice that has been completely cooked and dehydrated and can be reconstituted in boiling water. Precooked rice, to my taste, is very short on flavor.

MAKES 3 CUPS.

1 cup brown or white rice
Pinch of salt
1 teaspoon vegetable oil

1. In a medium saucepan, mix the rice, salt, oil, and 2 cups cold water and bring to a boil over high heat. Gently stir the rice, cover the pot, and reduce the heat to low.
2. Simmer about 15 minutes for white rice and 45 minutes for brown rice, or until the liquid is absorbed and the rice is dry and fluffy.

RISOTTO WITH DRIED MUSHROOMS

This Italian rice classic takes time and patience, but the results are sublime. Risotto must be made at the last minute, so I always invite my dinner guest into the kitchen so we can have a chance to talk for a good 30 minutes. Conversation flows while I stir the rice and we both inhale the earthy scent of wild mushrooms, Parmesan cheese, beef stock, and simmering rice.

You can make this risotto without the dried mushrooms, substituting chunks of prosciutto, ham, sun-dried tomatoes, sautéed onions and herbs, or whatever you like. You can also use chicken stock instead of beef. However you choose to make your risotto, there are two crucial ingredients: First, and most important, is the rice. Try to find a good Italian Arborio rice, a round, short grain that can hold up to the long cooking time required for a proper risotto. Second, you must use an authentic Parmigiano-Reggiano; imitation Parmesan just won't do.

SERVES 2 TO 4.

   ¹/₃ cup dried porcini, shiitake, chanterelle, or morel mushrooms
   2 to 2¹/₂ cups beef stock, preferably homemade (page 18)
   3 tablespoons butter
   ¹/₂ cup chopped onions
   Freshly ground black pepper
   1 cup raw rice (see headnote)
   ¹/₂ cup dry white wine, preferably Italian
   1 cup freshly grated Parmesan cheese (see headnote)
   3 tablespoons minced fresh parsley

1. Place the dried mushrooms in a bowl and cover with 1¹/₂ cups very warm water. Let soak for 30 minutes. Drain the mushrooms over another bowl, reserving the liquid. Dry the mushrooms on paper towels and thinly slice; set aside. Strain the remaining mushroom liquid and set aside.

2. Heat the stock over moderate heat until almost boiling.

3. In a medium heavy-bottomed saucepan, melt the butter over moderate heat. Sauté the onions with a generous grinding of pepper for about 8 minutes, until soft but not brown. Add the rice and stir to coat the kernels. Add the wine and let simmer, stirring frequently, for about a

minute. Add the sliced mushrooms and 1 cup of the reserved mushroom liquid. Stir frequently until the liquid is nearly evaporated. Add 1 cup of the hot beef stock and stir, stir, and stir until the stock has been incorporated. (Patience. Remember: I said it takes time.) Add the second cup of hot stock and continue stirring until the risotto is creamy and the rice is almost tender. Add the extra 1/2 cup if the rice is still chewy.

4. Remove the risotto from the heat and gently stir in 1/2 cup of the cheese and the parsley. Add more pepper if necessary. Cover and serve immediately with additional grated cheese on the side.

Risotto Cakes

In my kitchen, leftover risotto is not exactly a major problem. But it is so rich that occasionally even I will have leftovers. These cakes, a combination of cooked risotto, egg, cheese, and bread crumbs, make a wonderful first course, hors d'oeuvre, or light supper.

MAKES ABOUT 5 THREE-INCH CAKES.

> 1 cup cooked risotto
> 1 large egg, beaten
> 1/2 cup bread crumbs (page 46)
> 1/2 cup freshly grated Parmesan cheese
> 1 teaspoon crumbled dried basil, thyme, rosemary, or sage
> 1 tablespoon butter
> 1 tablespoon olive oil
> 1 tablespoon minced fresh parsley

1. In a bowl mix the risotto, beaten egg, 1/4 cup of the bread crumbs, and 1/4 cup of the grated cheese.

2. Place the remaining 1/4 cup of bread crumbs on a plate. Stir in the herbs and set aside.

3. Form the rice mixture into 3-inch cakes. Lightly coat both sides of the cakes with the bread crumbs. Set aside. (The cakes can be prepared ahead up to this point, wrapped in foil, and refrigerated for several hours before serving.)

4. In a large skillet, heat the butter and oil over moderate heat. Sauté the cakes about 3 minutes on each side, until golden brown and warm throughout. (Keep warm in a low oven if you're making a bunch.) Sprinkle the warm cakes with the remaining grated cheese and parsley and serve.

Spicy Oriental Rice Salad
with Tahini-Chile Vinaigrette

This recipe calls for quite a bit (5 cups) of leftover rice. You can easily cut the quantities in half should you have only a small amount of leftover rice on hand.

SERVES 4 TO 6.

The Vinaigrette:

2½ tablespoons tahini
1½ teaspoons minced fresh ginger, or 1 teaspoon powdered
4 tablespoons vegetable oil
2½ tablespoons wine vinegar
2½ tablespoons Chinese rice wine
1½ tablespoons sesame oil
½ to 1 teaspoon Chinese chile oil

The Salad:

5 cups cooked rice, preferably brown
2 scallions, thinly sliced
1 large carrot, chopped into small pieces
1 stalk celery, chopped into small pieces
1 cup thinly sliced water chestnuts, preferably fresh
12 mushrooms, thinly sliced
½ cup peanuts, walnuts, or pine nuts (optional)

1. Make the vinaigrette: Mix the tahini with the ginger in a medium bowl. Mix in the remaining ingredients, using only ½ teaspoon chile oil, and stir until smooth. Taste for seasoning. If you like an especially spicy salad, add the other ½ teaspoon of chile oil.

2. Assemble the salad: In a large bowl, break up any clumps in the rice. Mix in the scallions, carrots, celery, and water chestnuts. Gently mix in the vinaigrette until the entire salad is well coated. Mound the salad in the center of the bowl and scatter the raw mushrooms around the sides. Sprinkle the nuts on top, if desired.

Gingered Fried Rice with Chicken and Peanuts

The trick to really good fried rice is to cook the mixture over very high heat in a well-seasoned wok or frying pan. If the wok isn't hot enough the rice will stick.

This dish can be made using any leftover meat or poultry—it's particularly good with duck, pork, sausage, or turkey. Brown rice gives this dish a better texture, but the recipe also works with white rice.

SERVES 2 TO 4

1 tablespoon safflower oil
1 tablespoon minced fresh ginger
3 scallions, thinly sliced
1 cup sliced mushrooms
$1/2$ cup sliced celery
1 cup thinly sliced cooked chicken (see headnote)
$2^1/2$ cups cooked brown rice
$1/2$ cup unsalted shelled peanuts
2 eggs, beaten with 1 teaspoon sesame oil and $1/2$ teaspoon Chinese chile oil or Tabasco sauce
Soy sauce
Sesame oil

1. In a wok or a large skillet, heat the oil over high heat. Add $1/2$ of both the ginger and scallions and sauté a few seconds. Add the mushrooms and celery and sauté 2 minutes. Stir in the chicken and the remaining ginger and scallions and stir-fry for another minute.

2. Add the rice, being sure to break up any clumps, and cook for 3 minutes, stirring constantly to make sure the rice doesn't burn or stick to the bottom of the wok. Add the peanuts and the flavored egg mixture and cook 2 to 3 minutes, stirring constantly, or until the eggs are thoroughly cooked and incorporated into the rice. Serve with soy sauce and additional sesame oil on the side.

Fried Rice #2

Fried rice can incorporate all sorts of leftovers—cooked vegetables and bits of cooked meat, poultry, or pork. This version is unusually good for two reasons: first, the thick hoisin sauce that is served on top; and second, the sesame-oil-flavored omelette that's incorporated into the rice. Once you have all your ingredients ready, the dish will take only minutes to put together.

SERVES 2.

The Sauce:
2 tablespoons chicken stock (page 193)
1 tablespoon light soy sauce
1 teaspoon hoisin sauce
1 teaspoon Chinese rice wine, sake, or dry sherry

The Rice:
2 eggs
$^{1}/_{2}$ teaspoon sesame oil
2 teaspoons peanut or vegetable oil
3 scallions, thinly sliced
1 tablespoon chopped garlic
1 tablespoon chopped fresh ginger, or 1 teaspoon powdered
1 tablespoon Chinese fermented black beans, rinsed and chopped
About $^{1}/_{2}$ cup cubed cooked meat, poultry, or vegetables
2 cups cooked white or brown rice
1 cup mung bean sprouts
Dash hot Chinese chile paste, chile oil, or Tabasco sauce
Soy sauce
$1^{1}/_{2}$ tablespoons chopped fresh coriander (optional)

1. Make the sauce: Heat the chicken stock, soy sauce, hoisin sauce, and rice wine in a small saucepan over low heat until warm.
2. In a small bowl, beat the eggs with the sesame oil.
3. Heat a wok or large skillet over high heat. When hot, add 1 teaspoon of the oil. Add 1 tablespoon of the scallions and stir-fry for about 8 seconds. Add the eggs, let set about 10 seconds, then fold over like an omelette and cook another few seconds until set. Remove from the wok and cut the omelette into $^{1}/_{2}$-inch-wide strips; set aside.
4. Add the remaining teaspoon of oil to the hot wok. Stir in the

garlic and ginger for 5 seconds. Add 1 tablespoon of the scallions and the black beans and cooked meat or vegetables and stir-fry for another 10 seconds. Add the rice and stir constantly for 2 minutes. Add the sprouts, a dash of chile paste, and about a tablespoon of soy sauce. When the rice is warm throughout, gently add the omelette strips. Place the fried rice on a serving plate and top with the warm sauce, remaining scallions, and optional coriander.

■■■■■■■■■■■■■■■■■■■■■■■■■■■■■■■■■■■■■■

Curried Rice with Raisins and Slivered Almonds

Serve with broiled poultry, meats, fish, or vegetables. The curried rice is delicious garnished with grated coconut and a good mango chutney.

SERVES 2 TO 4

2 cups cooked rice
2 tablespoons butter
¹/₂ cup slivered almonds
¹/₂ cup raisins
1 tablespoon curry powder
1 teaspoon ground cumin
2 tablespoons fresh lemon juice
Freshly ground black pepper or cayenne

1. Heat the rice in a steamer or in a saucepan with a touch of water over low heat until warm, about 3 to 5 minutes.

2. In a small skillet, melt the butter over moderately low heat. Sauté the almonds until golden, about 2 to 3 minutes. Add the raisins, curry powder, and cumin and sauté 30 seconds.

3. Pour the curried nut butter over the warm rice, mix in the lemon juice, and season with pepper.

■■

Orange and Ginger Rice Pudding

Aaah, rice pudding. The ultimate comfort food, full of wonderful childhood memories. This version is very subtly flavored with orange and ginger—just enough to make the pudding special. You can turn this into a grown-up rice pudding by soaking the raisins in Grand Marnier (or for that matter, bourbon) and adding a dash of the liqueur to the egg and milk mixture.

SERVES 4 TO 6.

½ cup raisins
¼ cup orange juice or Grand Marnier
2 large eggs
1 cup milk
⅓ cup maple syrup or honey
1 teaspoon vanilla extract
1 teaspoon powdered ginger
1 teaspoon grated orange zest
½ teaspoon ground cinnamon
⅛ teaspoon grated nutmeg
2 cups cooked white rice*
2 tablespoons brown sugar mixed with 1 teaspoon ground cinnamon
1 cup heavy cream

1. Preheat the oven to 350 degrees.
2. Generously butter an 8-inch-square baking pan.
3. In a small bowl, soak the raisins in the orange juice or Grand Marnier for 20 minutes.
4. In a large bowl, vigorously whisk the eggs with the milk, maple syrup, and vanilla.
5. Drain the raisins and add to the mixture along with the ginger, orange zest, cinnamon, and nutmeg. Mix in the rice, stirring well to break up any clumps.
6. Pour into the prepared pan and bake 15 minutes. Remove from the oven and sprinkle with the brown sugar/cinnamon mixture. Bake another 10 minutes, or until the pudding is set.
7. Remove from the oven and serve hot, warm, or cold with heavy cream on top.

*Pudding can be made using only 1 cup of rice and halving all other ingredients.

MASTER RECIPE:

BAKED POTATOES

A baked potato is perfect food—simple, comforting, nutritious, and full of possibilities. I always end up cooking a few extra potatoes, because I love to have them around for making home fries, hash, salads, etc.

Also delicious are homemade potato chips (a low-fat version of French fries): very thinly slice baking potatoes and place on a lightly oiled baking sheet; brush with vegetable oil or melted butter, sprinkle with salt and pepper, and bake in a 375 degree oven until tender and golden brown, about 10 minutes on each side.

SERVES 2 TO 4.

4 medium baking potatoes

1. Preheat the oven to 350 degrees.
2. Scrub the potatoes well. Using a fork, pierce the flesh in several spots. Place in the preheated oven and bake until tender when pierced with a fork, about 40 minutes to 1 hour depending on the size. If you are in a rush, thread the potatoes onto a long skewer and bake. The skewer heats up the insides of the potatoes, causing them to cook more quickly.
3. Serve, piping hot, with a pat of butter, salt, and pepper. Of course there's always sour cream, chives, yogurt, grated cheese, and millions of other toppings as well.

BAKED SWEET POTATOES

The sweet potato comes from a different botanical family than the ordinary white potato. It is quite a bit sweeter, with a rich orange or yellowish flesh. Yams, which are yet another tuber, can be substituted for sweet potatoes.

Leftover sweet potato can be mashed and warmed with butter, maple syrup, a touch of cinnamon, and nutmeg, or added to soups and stews when a sweet flavor and meaty potato texture are desired.

SERVES 2.

2 large sweet potatoes

1. Preheat the oven to 375 degrees.
2. Pierce the potato with a knife in several places. Wrap in aluminum foil and bake for about 45 to 60 minutes, depending on the size, or until tender when pierced with a fork. Split and add a touch of butter and salt and pepper.

MASTER RECIPE:

MASHED POTATOES

SERVES 4.

4 large baking potatoes, peeled
About ½ cup milk
About 3 tablespoons butter
Salt
Freshly ground black pepper

1. Put the potatoes in a large pot of rapidly boiling water. Boil for about 10 to 15 minutes, depending on the size, or until soft when tested with a fork or knife.
2. Warm the milk over low heat.
3. Drain the potatoes. Mash them using a masher or large fork, or place in the container of a food processor and process until mashed but not pureed. (The hand method works best, because small, irregular chunks are an integral part of real homemade mashed potatoes.) Add the warm milk and butter and stir vigorously until incorporated. If the potatoes still seem dry, add another ¼ cup of milk and a tablespoon of butter. Season with salt and pepper and serve piping hot.

■■■
Garlicked Home Fries

Home fries—that coffee shop breakfast favorite—are nothing more than fried potatoes and onions seasoned with salt and pepper. But, as we all know, there are great home fries and terrible ones. There are several issues to consider. Should you cook the potatoes in butter or oil or both? Do you slice the potatoes lengthwise, cut them into cubes, or shred them German-style? Should the onions be sweet red ones or the pungent yellow variety? Will a skillet work as well as a griddle?

I have found that small cubes of potatoes (versus slices), chopped sweet red onion, lots of butter, finely chopped garlic, and a generous sprinkling of fresh or dried herbs produce melt-in-your-mouth home fries.

For the ultimate Sunday breakfast, serve with fried eggs, pan-fried tomato slices, baked beans, and thick slices of toasted homemade bread served with several flavors of fruit jelly and marmalade.

SERVES 2 TO 4.

> **3 tablespoons butter**
> **1 medium red onion, coarsely chopped**
> **1½ tablespoons minced garlic**
> **2 baked or boiled potatoes, cut into small cubes**
> **1½ teaspoons each chopped fresh rosemary, thyme, chives, and**
>   **basil, or 1 teaspoon each crumbled dried**
> **Generous grinding of fresh black pepper**

1. In a skillet or griddle that's large enough to hold all the potatoes without crowding, melt the butter over moderate heat. Add the onion and sauté about 5 minutes, until softened and beginning to turn golden brown. (Be careful not to let the onion burn.) Sprinkle in the garlic and stir.

2. Add the potatoes and herbs and sauté another 10 minutes, gently turning the potatoes every few minutes. (The trick is to let them brown on each side and then gently flip them over. The result you're looking for is potatoes with a golden brown crust.) Season to taste with pepper and additional herbs if needed.

■■

Shaker Potatoes

My friend Bill Bell taught me this one. It is loosely based on an old Shaker recipe.

SERVES 4.

> **5 tablespoons butter**
> **2 cups mashed potatoes**
> **1 cup cubed cheddar or Monterey Jack cheese**
> **1 medium onion, minced**
> **¹/₄ cup bread crumbs (page 46)**
> **4 tablespoons freshly grated Parmesan cheese**
> **Salt**
> **Freshly ground black pepper**

1. Preheat the oven to 350 degrees.
2. Grease a medium shallow ovenproof casserole with 1 tablespoon of butter; cut the remaining butter into small cubes. Spread the mashed potatoes in the casserole in an even layer. Press the cubed cheese into the potatoes. Spread the minced onion on top of the mixture and then sprinkle on the bread crumbs, grated Parmesan cheese, and salt and pepper to taste. Top with the butter cubes. (The recipe can be made several hours ahead up to this point. Cover and refrigerate until ready to bake.)
3. Bake casserole for 30 to 40 minutes, or until golden brown and hot throughout.

■■

Mashed Potatoes with Chorizo

Perfect for a cold winter's night. Serve with grilled veal or lamb chops, a mixed green salad, and a hearty red wine and feel the warmth.

SERVES 2 TO 4.

2 to 3 cups mashed potatoes
Salt
Freshly ground black pepper
1 fresh chorizo, linguica, or spicy Italian sausage, thinly sliced
Paprika
¹/₄ cup freshly grated Parmesan cheese, optional

1. Preheat the oven to 350 degrees.
2. Season the potatoes lightly with salt and pepper if needed and spread them over the bottom of a medium ovenproof casserole or shallow baking dish. Top with the sausage slices, paprika, and cheese if desired. Bake for 20 minutes, until the potatoes are warmed through and the sausages are cooked. Brown under the broiler for about a minute.

■■

Mashed Potato Cakes with Scallions

Serve with egg dishes, brisket or boiled meat, chicken, or game.

MAKES ABOUT 4 CAKES.

1 cup mashed potatoes, at room temperature
¹/₃ cup finely chopped scallions
1 tablespoon heavy cream
Salt
Freshly ground black pepper
1 tablespoon butter
1 tablespoon vegetable or safflower oil

1. In a bowl, mix the mashed potatoes, scallions, cream, and salt and pepper to taste.
2. Using your hands, form the potato mixture into 3-inch cakes. If the mixture is very sticky, lightly coat your hands with flour. Set aside. (The recipe can be prepared ahead up to this point and covered and refrigerated for several hours.)
3. In a medium skillet, heat the butter and oil over moderately high heat. Sauté the cakes about 2 to 4 minutes on each side, until crisp and golden brown.

Sautéed Baked Potato Slices

This simple recipe can be served with any type of poultry, beef, pork, or fish dish. It can be made into an elegant treat when topped with sour cream (or crème fraîche) and caviar and chopped chives.

SERVES 2.

  1 tablespoon butter
  1 teaspoon olive or vegetable oil
  1 cup thinly sliced baked or boiled potato, skin on
  Salt
  Freshly ground black pepper

1. Heat the butter and oil in a medium skillet over moderately high heat. Add the potato slices and sauté about 2 minutes on each side, or until golden brown. Season and serve hot.

John's New Potato Salad

SERVES 2 TO 4.

  4 tablespoons mayonnaise
  2 tablespoons wine vinegar
  1 teaspoon Dijon mustard
  Salt
  Freshly ground black pepper
  6 medium cooked new potatoes*
  1 stalk celery, chopped
  1 small onion, finely chopped
  3 tablespoons minced fresh parsley

*If the potatoes have butter and parsley on them or any other type of sauce, be sure to rinse and dry well.

1. In a medium serving bowl, combine the mayonnaise, vinegar, mustard, salt, and pepper.

2. If the new potatoes are small, slice them in half. If they are the larger variety, you may want to cut them in quarters. Add to the bowl, along with the celery, onion, and parsley, and mix gently. Taste for seasoning.

■■■

French-Style Potato Salad

This is a very basic dish, but one that is devoured every time. You can "dress" the recipe up by adding leftover cooked shrimp, chopped vegetables, or chopped hard-boiled eggs.

SERVES 2 TO 3.

1 1/2 tablespoons mayonnaise
1 tablespoon Dijon mustard
1 1/2 teaspoons paprika
2 tablespoons red or white wine vinegar
3 tablespoons olive oil
1 large baked potato, peeled and cubed, or 1 cup cubed boiled
   potatoes
2 scallions, sliced, or 1/2 small onion, finely chopped
1 1/2 tablespoons drained capers
Salt
Freshly ground black pepper

1. In a medium serving bowl, combine the mayonnaise, mustard, paprika, vinegar, and oil. Gently stir in the potatoes, scallions, and capers and season to taste.

███

Sweet Potato and Ham Croquettes

These croquettes—small deep-fried balls of mashed sweet potatoes, sautéed onions, nutmeg, and bits of chopped ham—are delicate morsels that melt in your mouth. Smooth, sweet, and sensuous.

You can use this as a Master Recipe and substitute all sorts of ingredients—mashed white potatoes instead of sweet potatoes, or turkey, duck, or goose instead of the ham. You could also omit the meat completely and simply make sweet potato and onion croquettes, or add bits of chopped vegetables to the mixture; peas are particularly good.

Serve these savory croquettes as an hors d'oeuvre, first course, garnish for roast poultry, meat, or game, or as a light main course for lunch or dinner.

The croquette mixture must chill for several hours, so plan your time accordingly.

MAKES ABOUT 12 TO 14 CROQUETTES.

> **1 tablespoon butter**
> **1 small onion, finely chopped**
> **Salt**
> **Freshly ground black pepper**
> **Grinding of fresh nutmeg**
> **1¹/₂ cups mashed sweet potato or white potato***
> **1 egg yolk**
> **1 tablespoon milk or heavy cream**
> **¹/₂ cup diced cooked ham (or turkey, duck, or goose)**
> **About 1 cup flour**
> **About 1 cup bread crumbs (page 46)**
> **2 eggs**
> **Peanut oil**

1. In a large skillet, melt the butter over moderate heat. Sauté the onion with a sprinkling of salt, pepper, and nutmeg for about 5 minutes, or until softened but not brown.

2. Place onion in a large bowl. Add the mashed potatoes, egg yolk, milk, and ham and mix together. Season generously with salt, pepper, and nutmeg.

---

*You can use leftover mashed potatoes or simply take a boiled or baked potato and mash it until somewhat smooth.

3. Cover and refrigerate the potato mixture for several hours, or overnight, until well chilled.

4. Place the flour on a large plate. Place the bread crumbs on another plate. Whisk the eggs in a bowl and season with salt and pepper.

5. To form the croquettes, take about a tablespoon of mixture in your hands and form into a ball. Roll the ball in the flour; remove and shake off excess. Dip into the egg and coat thoroughly, and then coat in the bread crumbs. Place the prepared croquettes on a large plate while you heat the oil.

6. Add enough peanut oil to a large skillet or deep-fat fryer to come 2½ inches up the side. Heat the oil to 375 degrees. (If you don't have a thermometer, simply add a tiny bit of bread crumbs or flour to the fat, and when it's ready it will sizzle vigorously.)

7. Fry the croquettes about 2 to 3 minutes, or until golden brown. (Be careful not to crowd the skillet.) Remove and drain on paper towels and serve immediately.

■■

Stephen's Spicy Sweet Potato and Chicken

This unusual spread has a good balance of sweetness (from the sweet potato) and spiciness (from the jalapeño peppers). Spoon it into a warm corn tortilla, with refried beans if you like, and roll it up. You can also accompany the dish with shredded lettuce, chopped tomatoes, and chopped onions.

SERVES 2.

1½ tablespoons olive oil
1 large cooked sweet potato, peeled and mashed, about 1½ cups
1 cup shredded cooked chicken or turkey
1 to 3 pickled jalapeño peppers or 1 fresh, chopped
Salt
4 corn tortillas

1. In a medium saucepan, heat the olive oil over moderately low heat. Add the mashed potato, the chicken, and half the peppers and heat through. Taste; if you want the mixture spicy add the remaining pepper. Season to taste with salt.

2. In a low oven, heat the tortillas for about 1 minute on each side, or until they are warm but not brittle. Serve the sweet potato mixture alongside or rolled up in the warm corn tortillas.

Potato Frittata

This is having your eggs and home fries all in one. You can also add any other vegetables you have on hand—carrots, eggplant, tomatoes, and so on—or any combination or herbs and spices.

SERVES 4.

1 tablespoon butter
1 tablespoon safflower oil
1 large onion, thinly sliced
1 zucchini, thinly sliced
1½ cups cubed cooked potatoes
2 tablespoons chopped fresh thyme, or 1 teaspoon dried crumbled
Freshly ground black pepper
5 eggs
Pinch of salt, optional
½ cup grated or very thinly sliced cheese: Parmesan, cheddar,
    Muenster, or a combination
2 tablespoons chopped fresh parsley

1. In a large ovenproof skillet or shallow casserole, melt the butter and oil over moderate heat. Sauté the onion for about 3 minutes. Add the zucchini and sauté until light brown. Add the potatoes, half the thyme, and the pepper. Cook over low heat for about 4 to 5 minutes.

2. Preheat the oven to 400 degrees.

3. In a bowl, vigorously beat the eggs with the remaining thyme, a light sprinkle of pepper and salt, and the cheese. Pour the eggs over the potato mixture in the skillet and cook for about 30 seconds. Place on the middle shelf of the oven and bake for about 15 to 20 minutes, or until the frittata puffs up like a soufflé and has a very light golden color. Sprinkle with the parsley and serve immediately.

French Fry Omelette

It sounds absurd, the idea of leftover french fries, but when you think about how many times you've left your plate full of fries, it starts to make sense. This idea—which reheats leftover french fries and folds them into a fluffy omelette—comes from chefs Phil and Varel McGuire of Portsmouth, New Hampshire. I am presenting this as a generic recipe, because the exact quantities depend on how many fries you have. You can also try it with leftover onion rings. Basically, figure on 1 cup leftover fries or onion rings to 4 eggs.

1. Cut fries into julienne strips (if you're working with onion rings, leave them whole). Reheat the fries by warming under the broiler or quickly sautéing in a touch of butter until golden brown.

2. Make an omelette and place the reheated fries inside before folding (you could also add some shredded cheese). Cook until the eggs are set, fold omelette in half, and serve with ketchup on the side and a very crisp green salad.

SEE ALSO:

6
PORK

MASTER RECIPES

LEFTOVER RECIPES

BAKED HAM

The most important ingredient in this recipe is the ham itself. Use a good smoked country ham, not one of those water-filled pink pieces of meat that passes for ham in most supermarkets. There are countless glazes and marinades for baked ham. I like to try a different one every time. Below, you'll find a master recipe along with a couple of variations; feel free to experiment.

I have not given specific baking instructions because each ham varies. A New England-style smoked country ham, for example, need only be cooked for about 12 minutes per pound, while a Southern, Kentucky-style, or Virginia ham often must be soaked first and then baked a bit longer; check with your butcher for exact instructions and cooking times.

SERVES 12 TO 15.

An 8- to 10-pound country ham, with bone
Whole cloves
2 cups apple cider
1 cup orange juice, preferably freshly squeezed
1 cup dry sherry

1. Using a sharp knife, make small X's in the top of the ham and insert a whole clove into each one. Place the ham in a large roasting pan. Pour the cider, orange juice, and sherry on top.* Cover, refrigerate, and let marinate at least 2 hours or preferably overnight, basting every few hours.

2. Bake according to butcher's instructions, basting the meat every 30 minutes or so. Add more cider or sherry if the juices at the bottom of the roasting pan dry up.

3. Let the ham sit about 15 minutes before serving.

*Other ideas: Instead of the cider, orange juice, and sherry, marinate the ham in 2 cups orange juice and 1 cup cassis (black currant liqueur); or 2 cups pineapple juice and 1 cup dark rum.

MASTER RECIPE:

ROAST PORK

SERVES 6.

1 center cut boneless loin of pork, about 3 1/2 pounds
Olive oil
6 garlic cloves, thinly sliced
1 tablespoon chopped fresh sage
1 tablespoon chopped fresh thyme
Freshly ground black pepper
1/2 cup white wine
1/2 cup apple cider or apple juice
2 tablespoons Dijon mustard
1/2 cup bread crumbs (page 46)

1. Preheat the oven to 400 degrees.
2. Place the pork in a large roasting pan and coat very lightly with olive oil. Using a sharp knife, cut several X's in the top of the pork and insert the garlic into the X's. Sprinkle the meat with the herbs and a generous grinding of pepper. Pour half the wine and cider over the roast.
3. Place the roast in the preheated oven and reduce the heat to 325 degrees. Add the remaining wine and cider if needed as the pan juices evaporate during the roasting time. Bake about 30 to 45 minutes per pound, or until the pork reaches an internal temperature of 150 degrees. The pork juices should be clear yellow and not pink. Fifteen minutes before the roast is done, use a pastry brush to spread the mustard over the top of the meat, then top with the bread crumbs. Bake until browned on top.
4. Let the roast sit at least 15 minutes before serving.

MASTER RECIPE:

SAUSAGES

Most sausages are loaded with fat. This simple cooking method—pricking the sausages, boiling them in water, and then sautéing in the natural fat—produces a crisp, golden brown sausage with a considerable amount of the fat removed.

Cooked sausages can be added to soups, stews, and casseroles, or reheated in a low oven and served with an assortment of mustards and dark breads. They are also excellent heated up in homemade white beans (page 253).

4 pork sausages: chorizo, sweet or hot Italian, linguica, etc.

1. Prick the sausages with a fork in several spots. Place in a shallow skillet and barely cover with cold water. Bring to a boil, reduce the heat, then let simmer until the water has evaporated. Raise the heat to medium and slowly brown the sausages in the fat that has escaped into the bottom of the skillet, about 5 to 8 minutes, depending on the size. Drain on paper towels and serve.

MASTER RECIPE:

HAM STOCK

MAKES ABOUT 8 CUPS.

**1 ham bone, with any remaining meat on the bone cut off and
   reserved
2 stalks celery, chopped
1 carrot, chopped
1 large onion or 2 small, quartered
4 fresh sage leaves, or ½ teaspoon crumbled dried
2 tablespoons chopped fresh basil, or 1 teaspoon crumbled dried
6 peppercorns
Sprig of fresh parsley
Pinch of salt**

1. Place the ham bone, celery, carrot, onion, sage leaves, basil, peppercorns, parsley, and salt (if the ham isn't too salty to begin with) in a large stockpot and add enough cold water to cover about three quarters of the bone. Bring to a boil over high heat. Reduce the heat to medium, cover partially, and simmer for about 1½ hours. Remove the cover and boil for 5 to 10 minutes over high heat to reduce the stock and intensify the flavor. Strain the stock over a large bowl and discard the bones and vegetables. Using a spoon, remove any grease that is floating on top of the stock. Use to make a soup. (See Hearty Vegetable Soup on page 154.) The stock can also be frozen.

CHINESE FOOD
OR . . .
WHAT TO DO WITH THAT COLD BROWN FOOD
IN WHITE PAPER CONTAINERS

Leftover Chinese food. What can you do with it? Heat it up in the wok? Throw it into the microwave? No! Everyone knows you eat it cold, straight from the little white container.

There is a better way. We had just dined at a mediocre Chinese restaurant in Portsmouth, N.H. (in New Hampshire there is no other kind of Chinese restaurant). The so-called Sichuan shrimp had been . . . shall we say, less than wonderful. The waitresses eyed our three-quarters-full plate and said, "Oh I see you're much too full to finish this all. I'll wrap it up and you can take it home." She seemed so genuine that we didn't have the heart to tell her we didn't eat it because it was bland and tasteless. There we were the next day with nothing in the refrigerator but the container of Sichuan shrimp with a layer of cold, semihard white rice. We were hungry, so I went to work.

What I discovered is that even mediocre Chinese food can be resurrected the next day if you add a few fresh ingredients and a little zing—this time it was in the form of Chinese chile paste.

My generic recipe for leftover Chinese food—be it shrimp, pork, vegetables, beef, or chicken—is as follows: Heat a large skillet or wok with a touch of vegetable or peanut oil. Add a clove of minced garlic and a teaspoon of minced fresh ginger (or powdered, if you must). Add the leftover rice (always ask for the leftover rice; it's also delicious in salads or fried rice—see recipes on pages 129, 130) and stir well to break up any clumps. Stir in the main course (you can even mix two main dishes together if you think they'd be compatible—like chicken with mixed Chinese vegetables and hot sautéed string beans) and stir-fry. Then add 1 teaspoon or more of any of the following: soy sauce, sesame oil, Chinese rice vinegar, or lemon or lime juice, or 1/2 to 1 teaspoon of black bean paste, chile oil, or chile paste. Experiment. Make the sauce go further by adding a tablespoon or two of water (or add a splash of rice wine) and simmer until the sauce thickens a bit. In the case of our Sichuan shrimp, they tasted far better the next day heated up in our wok than they did fresh from the restaurant's kitchen.

■■

Pasta e Fagioli
(Bean and Pasta Soup with Pork)

SERVES 2 TO 4 AS A MAIN COURSE AND 4 TO 6 AS A FIRST COURSE.

2 tablespoons olive oil
1 small onion, chopped
1 small carrot, chopped
1 stick celery, chopped
1 small zucchini, chopped
3 tablespoons chopped fresh rosemary, or 1½ tablespoons crumbled
  dried
6 tablespoons chopped fresh parsley
1 to 2 cups cubed cooked pork or ham
Bone from a ham, pork chops, or roast pork (optional)
⅔ cup chopped canned Italian tomatoes, or a simple meatless tomato
  sauce (page 239)
1 19-ounce can cannellini (white kidney) beans, drained, or 2½ cups
  homemade beans
3½ to 4½ cups homemade beef stock (page 18), or canned beef broth
Salt
Freshly ground black pepper
½ cup small tubular pasta
Freshly grated Parmesan cheese

1. In a large stockpot, heat the olive oil over moderate heat. Sauté
the onion until golden but not brown, about 6 minutes. Add the carrots,
celery, zucchini, half the rosemary, half the parsley, the pork, and any
bones; sauté for about 5 minutes. Add the tomatoes, reduce the heat a
bit, and simmer an additional 10 minutes. Add the drained beans and
3½ cups of stock and let the soup come to a gentle boil.

2. Scoop up about ½ cup of the beans and mash them in a bowl or
through a food mill. Return the mashed beans to the stockpot. Taste for
seasoning and add salt and pepper as needed.

3. Add the pasta—6 ounces if you want the soup to be only fairly
thick and all 8 ounces if you want it very thick and hearty. Cook until
the pasta is almost tender and remove the soup from the heat. (The
pasta will continue cooking.) If, at any point, the soup gets too thick
because the pasta is absorbing too much liquid, add another cup of stock
as needed.

4. Sprinkle the remaining rosemary and parsley over each soup
bowl and pass the cheese separately.

Hearty Vegetable Soup with Ham

There are many versions of minestrone, the classic Italian soup, all of which make use of fresh garden vegetables in a savory herb-laced broth. This is a particularly thick and hearty version that, served along with a green salad, a warm loaf of crusty bread, and a cold bottle of dry white wine, makes an excellent main course.

The secret to all soups is a good stock. This soup will work well with ham, veal, beef, even chicken stock. Be sure to reserve any meat remaining on the bones when you make the stock. This can be added to the soup just before serving.

Don't be put off by the number of ingredients called for in this soup. If you have beans and broccoli on hand but don't have green pepper and celery, just proceed without them. Also, this is a great opportunity to use up any leftover or not-quite-in-their-prime vegetables that might be hanging around.

SERVES 4 TO 6.

2 tablespoons olive oil
2 large garlic cloves, minced
2 leeks (white and light green part), cut lengthwise, rinsed well, and
    cut into 1 1/2-inch pieces (optional)
1 large onion or 2 small, chopped
1 1/2 cups chopped ripe or canned tomatoes
1 tablespoon chopped fresh thyme, or 1 teaspoon crumbled dried
1 tablespoon chopped fresh rosemary, or 1 teaspoon crumbled dried
4 cups chopped assorted vegetables (carrots, celery, asparagus,
    parsnips, bell peppers, broccoli, zucchini, etc.)
1 bay leaf
6 to 7 cups ham stock (see headnote), with any bits of meat from the
    bone with which the stock was made (page 151)
1 cup elbow macaroni, orzo, or other small pasta
1 19-ounce can cannellini beans, drained, or 2 cups homemade beans
    (page 253)
1 1/2 teaspoons chopped fresh sage, or 1/2 teaspoon crumbled dried
2 tablespoons chopped fresh basil, or 1 1/2 teaspoons crumbled dried
2 tablespoons chopped fresh dill
2 tablespoons chopped fresh Italian parsley
Salt

Freshly ground black pepper
Freshly grated Parmesan cheese

1. In a large soup pot, heat the oil over moderate heat. Sauté the garlic, leeks, and onion for 5 minutes. Add the tomatoes, thyme, and rosemary and simmer 5 minutes. Add the vegetables, the bay leaf, and 6 cups of the stock. Cover and let simmer for about 5 minutes.

2. Add the macaroni or orzo, the beans, herbs, and a dash of salt and pepper. Simmer the soup for 15 minutes. Taste the pasta; it should be tender. If the soup gets too thick as the pasta cooks, add the remaining cup of stock. Add any bits of meat left on the bone you used to make the stock.

3. Taste the broth for seasoning and adjust as needed. The soup should be rather thick. Serve with grated Parmesan cheese on the side and with bruschette or crostini (page 48).

Corn and Ham Chowder

SERVES 6.

1 tablespoon butter
1 teaspoon vegetable oil
1 medium onion, diced
2 shallots, diced
³/₄ cup diced cooked ham
3 cups peeled and cubed raw potatoes
¹/₂ bay leaf
3 tablespoons chopped fresh parsley
Salt
Freshly ground black pepper
3 cups milk
4 cups fresh corn, cut from about 8 medium cobs, or 4 cups frozen
2 tablespoons flour
¹/₄ cup chopped fresh basil
Butter
Sweet Hungarian paprika

1. In a large pot, melt the butter and oil over moderate heat. Sauté the onion and shallots for 5 minutes, or until softened but not brown. Add the ham and cook an additional 2 minutes, stirring occasionally.

2. Add the potatoes, 2 cups water, bay leaf, parsley, salt, and pepper. Bring to a boil over high heat, reduce the heat, and let simmer about 30 minutes, or until the potatoes are *just* tender.

3. Meanwhile warm the milk in a saucepan over moderately low heat.

4. Add the warm milk and the corn to the chowder and stir well.

5. Put the flour in a small bowl. Take 3 to 4 tablespoons of the hot broth from the pot and mix well with the flour to create a paste. Slowly add the flour paste to the pot, whisking to create a smooth soup. Let the soup come to a simmer and cook about 3 to 5 minutes, or until the soup is thickened and the corn is cooked but not soft. Remove from the heat and stir in the basil. Season with salt and pepper to taste.

6. Put a small cube of butter in each soup bowl, pour in the piping hot soup, and top with a sprinkling of paprika.

Sausage, Eggplant, and White Bean Stew

This hearty stew is also delicious made with leftover pork, ham, duck, or chicken. Serve with boiled potatoes.

SERVES 2 TO 4.

> **2 tablespoons olive oil**
> **3 garlic cloves, minced**
> **2 large onions, thinly sliced**
> **3 small baby white or purple eggplants, cut into quarters**
> **2 large green bell peppers, seeded and cut into thick slices**
> **Salt**
> **Freshly ground black pepper**
> **1½ tablespoons chopped fresh thyme, or 1 teaspoon crumbled dried**
> **1½ tablespoons chopped fresh basil, or 1 teaspoon crumbled dried**
> **1 19-ounce can cannellini beans, drained and rinsed, or 2½ cups**
>   **homemade beans**
> **1½ cups chopped fresh or canned tomatoes**
> **½ fresh chile pepper, chopped, or Tabasco sauce**
> **½ cup red wine**
> **1 bay leaf**
> **1½ cups sliced cooked sausage**

1. In a medium casserole, heat the oil over moderately low heat. Add the garlic and onions and cook for about 5 minutes, until golden and softened but not brown. Add the eggplant, peppers, salt, pepper, thyme, and basil and sauté for about 8 to 10 minutes. Add the beans, tomatoes, chile pepper, red wine, and bay leaf. Raise the heat for about 5 minutes, until the tomatoes have softened.

2. Stir in the cooked sausage and simmer for about 1 to 2 minutes, or until the sausage is heated throughout. Remove bay leaf.

■■

Pork and Bean Salad with Cumin and Mint Vinaigrette

Serve this unusual salad with a bowl of plain yogurt, warm triangles of pita bread, and crisp lettuce leaves.

SERVES 4.

The Salad:
 2 cups cooked black beans (page 253)
 1 cup cubed cooked pork
 1 cup cubed ripe tomatoes
 ³/₄ cup chopped scallions

The Vinaigrette:
 1 teaspoon ground cumin
 ¹/₃ cup coarsely chopped fresh mint
 ¹/₂ to 1 teaspoon chopped* dried red chile pepper
 2 tablespoons red wine vinegar
 1¹/₂ tablespoons fresh lemon juice
 5 tablespoons olive oil
 Salt
 Fresh mint leaves, for garnish
 Lettuce leaves
 ¹/₂ cup yogurt

1. Assemble the salad: In a medium serving bowl, mix the beans, pork, tomatoes, and scallions and set aside.
2. Make the vinaigrette: In a small bowl, mix the cumin, mint, and chile pepper. Whisk in the vinegar, lemon juice, and oil and season to taste, adding more chile pepper and salt as needed.
3. Add the vinaigrette to the salad, toss well, and let marinate in the refrigerator for at least 1 hour. Garnish with fresh mint leaves.
4. Place a spoonful of salad inside a lettuce leaf, top with a dollop of yogurt, and roll up like a cone. Eat accompanied by warm pita bread.

*Start by adding ¹/₂ teaspoon of chile and taste the vinaigrette. If you like it very spicy, add the remaining chile. Don't be concerned if the vinaigrette seems too spicy; once it's mixed with the other ingredients, its fire will mellow.

Summer Greens with Ham, Olives, Egg Wedges, and Zucchini with a Parmesan Cheese Vinaigrette

This salad is a wonderful combination of colors, flavors, and textures. The tiny egg wedges that border the platter are reminiscent of a summer sun.

SERVES 4.

The Salad:

4 hard-boiled eggs, peeled and cooled
About ³/₄ pound mixed summer greens (about 5 well-packed cups, a combination of two or three of the following: red and green leaf lettuce, mâche, arugula, dandelion greens, watercress, or sorrel)
1 cup tiny black and green French Niçoise olives
1¹/₂ cups julienne strips tiny young zucchini
¹/₂ pound ham, cut into julienne strips

The Vinaigrette:

1 teaspoon Dijon mustard
3 tablespoons white wine vinegar
¹/₃ cup good olive oil
Salt
Generous grinding of black pepper
¹/₃ cup fresh finely grated Parmesan cheese

1. Make the salad: Slice each egg into 8 wedges and set aside.
2. Place the greens in the center of a large serving platter and the eggs around the border. Sprinkle the olives inside the egg border. Place the zucchini strips in a line across the center of the lettuce and sprinkle the ham on top.
3. Make the vinaigrette: Mix the mustard and vinegar in a medium bowl. Whisk in the olive oil and season to taste. Add the cheese and spoon the dressing over the salad.

A Croque Monsieur Salad

I'll never forget my first trip to Paris. My memories are glossy, like French postcards. Everything was so exotic, so European—which in my 19-year-old vocabulary meant it was far superior to anything American. And everything I ate was *the best* thing I had ever tasted. (Even the hot dogs stuffed into a crusty baguette and smeared with Dijon mustard.)

One afternoon I was walking outside the Louvre when I saw a young woman making these incredible-looking grilled cheese and ham sandwiches on long, thin loaves of French bread. My first Croque Monsieur was an experience—the very best grilled ham and cheese I'd ever come across.

When I made this salad using cooked ham and just-melted cheese it reminded me of that first Croque Monsieur, *sans* bread. Serve this with a good crusty loaf of French bread and a bottle of dry white French wine.

SERVES 2 TO 4.

The Lemon-Basil Vinaigrette:
3 tablespoons olive oil
1 1/2 tablespoons red wine vinegar
Juice of 1/4 lemon
1/2 teaspoon Dijon mustard
1/4 cup chopped fresh basil, or 1 tablespoon crumbled dried
Pinch of sugar
Grinding of black pepper

The Salad:
1/2 teaspoon olive oil
1/2 teaspoon butter
3 garlic cloves, minced
1 cup julienne strips cooked ham
1 1/2 tablespoons freshly grated Parmesan cheese
4 cups mixed greens (spinach, red leaf lettuce, arugula, etc.)
Nasturtium flowers for garnish (optional)
Croutons (page 47)

1. Prepare the vinaigrette: In a small bowl, whisk together all the ingredients until smooth. Set aside.

2. Prepare the salad: In a small skillet, heat the oil and butter over

low heat. Add the garlic and sauté 10 seconds. Add the ham and sauté for another 10 seconds. Off the heat, add the grated cheese.

3. Place the mixed greens in a salad bowl or plate and top with the ham mixture. Garnish with the nasturtium flowers and drizzle the vinaigrette on top. Top with croutons.

■■■

Pork Salad with Mustard-Soy Sauce

You can add all sorts of food you might happen to find in the refrigerator to fill this salad out—hard-boiled egg wedges, anchovy filets, black olives, red grapes, celery sticks, or cooked vegetables, for example. Serve with warm toast triangles.

SERVES 4.

The Salad:
About 2 cups mixed greens
8 slices cooked loin of pork, at room temperature
Red bell pepper, seeded and cut into thick slices

The Vinaigrette:
2 tablespoons Dijon mustard
1½ teaspoons soy sauce
1 tablespoon fresh lemon juice
1 tablespoon wine vinegar
3½ tablespoons olive oil
Freshly ground black pepper

1. Assemble the salad: Arrange the greens in the center of the plate and surround with the pork and pepper slices.

2. Prepare the vinaigrette: In a small bowl, mix the mustard with the soy sauce, lemon juice, and vinegar. Whisk in the olive oil and season with pepper. Drizzle over the pork and greens.

Chinese Pork and Cabbage Salad

SERVES 4.

The Salad:

2 cups julienne strips cooked pork loin

2 cups very thinly sliced Chinese cabbage or red cabbage

1 small tart apple, peeled, cored, and sliced into julienne strips

1/2 cup mung bean sprouts

The Vinaigrette:

1 teaspoon chopped garlic

1 1/2 teaspoons chopped fresh ginger

1 tablespoon light soy sauce

1 1/2 tablespoons sesame oil

4 tablespoons red wine vinegar

6 tablespoons olive oil

Freshly ground black pepper

Rice cakes

1. Assemble the salad: Mix the pork, cabbage, apples, and sprouts on a serving plate or in a bowl.

2. Make the vinaigrette: In a small bowl, mix the garlic, ginger, soy sauce, and sesame oil. Whisk in the vinegar and oil and season with pepper. Add more soy sauce if you want a saltier vinaigrette.

3. Toss the vinaigrette with the salad and serve at room temperature with crispy rice cakes.

J.R.'s Succotash with Ham

This is a light summer dish in which the ham highlights the fresh flavors of the vegetables without overwhelming them. The recipe can easily be doubled or tripled to serve a crowd.

SERVES 2.

> 1/2 pound green beans, trimmed and cut into 1/2-inch pieces
> 2 large ears fresh or frozen corn
> 1 1/2 tablespoons butter
> 3 shallots, chopped
> 1/2 green bell pepper, seeded and diced
> 1/3 cup diced cooked smoked ham
> 1 1/2 tablespoons chopped fresh thyme
> Freshly ground black pepper

1. Place about an inch of water in the bottom of a steamer and bring to a boil. Steam beans for 3 minutes. Meanwhile, using a sharp knife, cut the corn kernels off the cob. Add the corn and steam 1 minute. Refresh under cold running water and drain.

2. In a medium skillet, melt 1 tablespoon of the butter over moderate heat. Sauté the shallots until translucent, about 3 minutes. Add the green pepper, ham, and thyme and sauté 2 minutes. Add the steamed vegetables and toss to warm. Transfer to a serving bowl and add the remaining 1/2 tablespoon of butter and a grinding of pepper.

■■

Leek, Ham, and Basil Tart

This tart should not be served straight from the oven. Let it sit for at least 10 minutes before serving.

SERVES 4 TO 6.

The Crust:
1¹/₂ cups flour
Pinch of salt
5¹/₂ tablespoons butter, chilled
3 tablespoons vegetable shortening
About 3 tablespoons ice-cold water

The Filling:
3 medium leeks
2 tablespoons olive oil
¹/₂ tablespoon butter
4 garlic cloves, minced
1 cup cubed cooked ham or pork
¹/₃ cup shredded fresh basil
Salt
Freshly ground black pepper
2 eggs
1 cup heavy cream
¹/₄ cup freshly grated Parmesan cheese
Small cluster of basil leaves for garnish (optional)

1. Prepare the crust: Sift the flour and salt into a large bowl. Cut the butter and shortening into small pieces and, using 2 kitchen knives (or your hands), work the butter into the flour until it resembles bread crumbs. Make a well in the center of the flour and add about 2¹/₂ tablespoons of the water. Work into the pastry, adding more water if needed to form a smooth ball of dough. Shape into a ball, wrap, and chill for at least 1 hour.

2. Remove the dough from the refrigerator. Roll it out to fit a 9-inch fluted tart (or quiche) pan with a removable bottom. Line the tart pan and trim the edges even with the top of the pan. Chill in the refrigerator for 30 minutes.

3. Preheat the oven to 400 degrees.

4. Prepare the filling: Cut the leeks lengthwise and wash under cold

water to remove any dirt caught in the layers. Cut into ½-inch pieces, using only 2 inches of green. (You should have about 3 cups of leeks.)

5. In a large skillet, heat the olive oil and butter over moderate heat. Sauté the garlic and leeks for about 5 minutes. Add the ham, basil, salt, and pepper and sauté another 2 to 3 minutes. Remove from the heat and let cool.

6. In a large bowl, whisk together the eggs, cream, and grated cheese. Gently stir in the cooled leek/ham mixture. Spoon the filling into the crust, place the tart in the preheated oven, and bake for 10 minutes. Reduce the heat to 325 degrees and bake an additional 50 minutes.

■■■

Breakfast Ham Slices in Caramelized Maple Butter

This is a variation on an old breakfast favorite. Serve with fried eggs and toast, or pancakes, waffles, or French toast.

SERVES 1 TO 2.

> **1 tablespoon butter**
> **4 thin slices cooked country ham**
> **1 to 1½ tablespoons maple syrup**

1. In a medium skillet, melt the butter over moderate heat. Sauté the ham slices about 1 minute. Turn over and drizzle the maple syrup on top. Let cook for another minute, until the maple syrup has caramelized slightly.

■■

Braised Escarole with Ham

Escarole, a slightly bitter green favored by Italian cooks, is excellent combined with the smoky flavor of ham. Serve with grilled veal or lamb chops or a hearty pasta.

SERVES 2 TO 4.

1 medium head escarole
2 tablespoons olive oil
1 small onion, chopped
2 garlic cloves, minced
1 cup chicken stock (page 193)
²/₃ cup diced cooked ham
Salt
Freshly ground black pepper
Freshly grated Parmesan cheese

1. Rinse the escarole leaves under cold running water to remove all dirt. Drain and shred the leaves.
2. In a large skillet, heat the olive oil over moderate heat. Add the onion and garlic and sauté about 5 minutes, until golden brown. Add the escarole leaves and sauté about 4 to 5 minutes, or until the leaves have wilted slightly. Stir in the chicken stock, lower the heat, and cover the skillet. Cook for 10 minutes, stirring occasionally. Remove the top, stir in the ham, and cook an additional minute or two. Season with salt and pepper. Serve hot with grated Parmesan cheese on the side.

Scalloped Potatoes with Ham

Whenever my friend Karen Frillmann was served baked ham as a child, this would be the dish that followed the next day. Her mother, Edna, would then use the ham bone to make soup.

The dish can be made ahead of time and baked just before serving.

SERVES 4.

3 tablespoons butter
4 medium raw potatoes, about 1 1/2 pounds, peeled and thinly sliced
2 small onions, thinly sliced
1/2 pound thinly sliced cooked country ham or cooked pork
2 tablespoons flour
Salt
Freshly ground black pepper
1 cup milk
2 tablespoons heavy cream
Paprika

1. Preheat the oven to 400 degrees.
2. Grease the bottom of a 10- to 12-inch ovenproof skillet or shallow casserole with 1 tablespoon of the butter. Place half the potatoes along the bottom of the skillet, overlapping them slightly. Sprinkle half the onions on top. Layer the ham over the onions and sprinkle with the remaining onions. Scatter the flour and some salt and pepper on top. Dot 1 tablespoon of butter over that layer and add the remaining potatoes over that. Pour the milk and cream over the potatoes, dot with the remaining tablespoon of butter, and add a grinding of fresh pepper and a generous sprinkle of paprika. (The dish can be made ahead up to this point.)
3. Place the dish on a cookie sheet in the preheated oven. Bake for 15 minutes, reduce the heat to 300 degrees, and bake an additional hour. After about 30 minutes of baking, tilt the dish gently and baste with the milk.

Medallions of Pork with Braised Fennel
and Apple-Mustard Wine Sauce

The licorice (or anise) flavor of fresh fennel complements the taste of pork beautifully. Serve this hearty dish with pan-fried potatoes and a bottle of cold cider or dry white wine.

SERVES 2.

The Pork and Fennel:
    1 head fresh fennel or celery
    1 1/2 tablespoons olive oil
    1 medium onion, thinly sliced
    1 teaspoon butter
    4 1-inch-thick slices cooked pork loin
    1 teaspoon chopped fresh thyme, or 1/2 teaspoon crumbled dried
    Freshly ground black pepper

The Sauce:
    1 teaspoon flour
    1/3 cup dry white wine
    1 teaspoon Dijon mustard
    1 1/2 tablespoons apple cider
    2 teaspoons pork essence from the pan drippings, or beef stock
    1/8 teaspoon chopped or crushed fennel seeds (optional)
    1 1/2 tablespoons heavy cream
    Few sprigs fresh thyme, for garnish (optional)

1. Cut the head off the fennel. Cut the bulb in half lengthwise, remove core, and cut into thin slices. (If using celery, cut off the tops and the very ends of the spears. Cut into 1 1/2-inch-thick slices.)
2. Put 1 tablespoon of the oil in a large saucepan. Add the fennel, onion, and 3/4 cup water; bring to a boil over high heat. Reduce the heat and let the vegetables simmer until they are somewhat softened but still crisp and the water has evaporated, about 20 to 25 minutes. If the water has not evaporated and the fennel is soft, simply blot the remaining water up with paper towels or drain it. Place the fennel and onion around the edge of a serving plate; cover and keep warm in a 200 degree oven.
3. Meanwhile, add the butter and remaining oil to the skillet and

place over moderate heat. Add the pork and sauté 1 minute on each side, sprinkling with the thyme and a generous amount of black pepper. Remove the pork and place in the center of the plate.

4. Prepare the sauce: Heat the fat that remains in the skillet. Sprinkle in the flour and let cook for a few seconds. Add the wine, mustard, cider, pork drippings, and optional fennel seeds. Let simmer over moderately high heat for about 2 minutes. Add the cream and simmer another minute and pour over the pork. Garnish with fresh thyme.

■■

Pork in a Caper Cream Sauce

It only takes about 10 minutes to put this dish together from start to finish. Serve with roast potatoes or buttered noodles and a watercress salad. This dish is also delicious made with thick slices of cooked turkey or chicken.

SERVES 2.

> 1 teaspoon olive or vegetable oil
> 1 teaspoon butter
> 4 1-inch-thick slices of cooked pork loin, ham, or leftover pork chops cut off the bone
> 1 tablespoon chopped fresh dill
> 2 tablespoons chopped fresh parsley
> 1/2 cup heavy cream
> 1 teaspoon Dijon mustard
> 1/2 teaspoon tomato paste
> 2 tablespoons drained capers
> Salt
> Freshly ground black pepper

1. In a medium skillet, heat the oil and butter over moderate heat. Add the pork and sauté about 1 minute. Flip to the other side, and add the dill and half the parsley.

2. Gently whisk in the cream, mustard, and tomato paste and let simmer about 3 to 5 minutes, or until thick enough to coat the back of a spoon. Add the capers and season to taste. Scatter the remaining parsley on top.

Spinach Fusilli in a Ham, Zucchini, Cream Sauce

SERVES 2.

The Pasta:

2$\frac{1}{2}$ cups fresh or dry spinach or plain fusilli, about $\frac{1}{2}$ pound (or any large shaped pasta)

The Sauce:

1 tablespoon olive oil
1 tablespoon butter
1 small onion, finely chopped
1 garlic clove, minced
1 small zucchini, diced, about 1 cup
$\frac{1}{2}$ cup diced cooked ham or pork
1 teaspoon chopped fresh thyme, or $\frac{1}{2}$ teaspoon crumbled dried
$\frac{1}{2}$ cup heavy cream
Salt
Freshly ground black pepper
2 to 3 tablespoons chopped fresh Italian parsley
About $\frac{1}{2}$ cup freshly grated Parmesan cheese

1. In a large pot of lightly salted boiling water, cook the pasta for about 10 to 12 minutes if dry and about 2 minutes if fresh, or until tender.
2. While the pasta cooks, make the sauce: In a medium skillet, heat the oil and butter over moderate heat. Sauté the onion and garlic until translucent, about 2 minutes. Add zucchini and cook about 4 minutes, until brown. Stir in the ham and thyme and sauté 1 minute. Reduce the heat to low and add the cream. Let simmer 1 to 2 minutes, until thickened. Add salt and pepper to taste.
3. Drain the pasta and toss thoroughly with the sauce. Sprinkle parsley on top. Pass the grated cheese separately.

Pork, Pea, and Tomato Sauce

Serve this sauce on top of buttered noodles or with rice mixed with lots of butter and grated Parmesan cheese.

SERVES 2.

> 1 1/2 tablespoons olive oil
> 1 1/2 tablespoons butter
> 1 small onion, chopped
> 1 1/2 tablespoons chopped fresh sage, or 1 1/2 teaspoons crumbled
>   dried
> 1 cup cubed cooked pork or ham
> 1 cup fresh or frozen green peas
> 4 teaspoons tomato paste diluted with 1/2 cup water
> Salt
> Freshly ground black pepper

1. In a medium saucepan, heat the oil and butter over moderate heat. Sauté the onion until soft but not brown, about 5 minutes.

2. Add the sage, pork, peas, diluted tomato paste, salt, and pepper. Cook, uncovered, over low heat for about 20 minutes. Makes enough to sauce 1 cup cooked rice or 1/4 pound cooked pasta.

■■■

Ham, Cheese, and Herb Baguette

This is a wonderful recipe for people who like to bake bread but don't have time for all the rising and punching down that goes along with most yeast breads. This French-style loaf can be made from start to finish in a little over an hour. It's a hearty loaf that is delicious sliced and lightly toasted and served with soups, stews, and salads. The ham adds a pleasing smoky flavor.

SERVES 8. MAKES 2 LOAVES.

1 1/2 tablespoons active dry yeast
1 1/2 cups warm water
1 tablespoon honey
About 4 cups unbleached white flour
1/2 teaspoon salt (optional)
4 tablespoons olive oil
1 1/2 cups cubed cooked ham or pork
1/2 cup freshly grated Parmesan cheese
2 teaspoons chopped fresh rosemary, or 1 teaspoon crumbled dried
2 teaspoons chopped fresh thyme, or 1 teaspoon crumbled dried
2 teaspoons chopped fresh sage, or 1 teaspoon crumbled dried
Generous grinding of black pepper

1. Place the yeast in a large mixing bowl. Mix in the warm water and honey and set aside in a warm spot for about 10 minutes, or until the yeast is dissolved and begins bubbling. (If the yeast does not bubble it is probably dead; begin again using fresh yeast.) Gradually sift the flour and salt into the yeast mixture, stirring constantly until the dough begins to pull away from the sides of the bowl.

2. Sprinkle some flour over a working surface and gently knead the dough for several minutes. Cut the dough in half and roll out one half into a rectangle (like a rectangular pizza), about 14 inches by 10 inches. Brush the dough with 1 1/2 tablespoons of the olive oil. Scatter half the ham over the surface, pressing it gently into the dough. Sprinkle half the cheese on top and scatter half the herbs and a generous grinding of fresh black pepper over the dough. Using your hands, gently roll the dough lengthwise, into the shape of a long cigar. Lightly seal the edges of the dough. Place in a well-greased French bread pan (or on a well-greased cookie sheet) and cover with a clean tea towel.

3. Preheat the oven to 450 degrees.

4. Make the second loaf. Place the two loaves of bread in a dry, warm spot and let them sit, covered, for 15 minutes.

5. Just before baking, lightly brush the loaves with the remaining 1 tablespoon of olive oil. Place in the middle shelf of the hot oven and bake 20 to 25 minutes, or until the bread has a golden brown crust and sounds hollow when tapped on the bottom.

CHEESE—WHAT TO DO WITH ALL THOSE RINDS AND THIN LITTLE LEFTOVER PIECES

The cheese drawer in our refrigerator is always filled with little bits and pieces of leftover cheese—the rind from a hunk of Parmesan, a hardened piece of cheddar, the end bit of a Camembert or Brie. What follows are some suggestions for using these odds and ends of cheese:

➤Quiche is a great way to use up bits of leftover cheese—be it cheddar, blue cheese, Roquefort, Gorgonzola, Camembert or Brie, cream or cottage cheese. See recipe on page 175.

➤Grate leftover cheese and freeze in a covered jar or plastic bag—use for quiche, or as a topping for soups, stews, casseroles, pizzas, sandwiches, or savory pies.

➤Save the rind from a hunk of Parmesan cheese to add flavor to a minestrone, vegetable, or meat-based soup. The rind is surprisingly full of flavor and, with authentic Parmigiano-Reggiano selling for nearly $11 a pound, you might as well get every last bit of flavor.

■■■

Quiche Lorraine
(Cheese and Bacon Quiche)

This is a basic recipe for foolproof quiche. You can alter the recipe depending on the leftovers you have at hand. Add pieces of cooked zucchini with slivers of goat cheese, or peas and blue cheese, or broccoli, tomato, and smoked mozzarella. You can omit the bacon or ham and make this an all-cheese, or cheese and vegetable quiche. Use your imagination.

SERVES 4 TO 6.

The Pastry:
1½ cups flour
½ teaspoon salt
12 tablespoons (1½ sticks) butter
2 to 3 tablespoons ice-cold water

The Quiche:
6 slices bacon, or ½ cup cubed cooked ham or prosciutto
1 tablespoon olive oil
1 tablespoon butter
3 onions, thinly sliced
3 eggs
1 cup heavy cream
½ cup sour cream
1 tablespoon chopped fresh basil, or ½ tablespoon crumbled dried
1½ tablespoons chopped fresh dill or thyme, or ½ tablespoon
   crumbled dried
Salt
Freshly ground black pepper
2 cups assorted grated cheeses (see headnote)

1. Make the pastry: Mix the flour and salt in a bowl. Add the butter, cut into small pieces, and, using 2 knives, cut it into the flour until the mixture resembles bread crumbs. Add enough water to hold the dough together. Knead with your hands until it forms a ball. Flatten, wrap, and chill for at least 2 hours.

2. Make the quiche filling: Sauté the bacon over moderate heat until golden and crisp. Drain and crumble into small pieces. Set aside.

3. Discard all but 1 teaspoon of the bacon fat. Add the olive oil and

(continued)

butter and warm over moderately low heat. Sauté the onions slowly for about 15 minutes, until golden brown.

4. Preheat the oven to 375 degrees.

5. In a bowl beat the eggs, cream, sour cream, herbs, salt, and pepper. Add the grated cheese, onions, the reserved bacon (or ham), and any leftover vegetables.

6. Roll out the dough and fit into a 10-inch lightly buttered tart pan with removable bottom. Spoon in the filling and gently level it with the back of the spoon.

7. Bake about 40 minutes, or until a toothpick comes out clean.

SEE ALSO:

OPEN-FACED ROAST BEEF SANDWICH WITH A SHALLOT-MUSTARD-CREAM
    SAUCE   21
    Substitute 6 slices cooked pork for the beef.
MEXICAN STEAK SANDWICH WITH AVOCADO CREAM   22
    Substitute 8 thin slices cooked pork for the beef.
THAI BEEF SALAD   27
    Substitute 1 cup thinly sliced cooked pork for the beef.
MEDALLION OF BEEF SALAD WITH HORSERADISH SAUCE   28
    Substitute 10 thin slices cooked pork for the beef.
CORNED BEEF AND ORIENTAL CABBAGE SALAD   29
    Substitute 4 to 6 thin slices cooked pork for the corned beef.
STIR-FRIED STEAK WITH BROCCOLI, CASHEWS, AND SPICY NUT SAUCE   30
    Substitute 8 thin slices cooked pork for the steak.
MA PO DOFU (SPICY SICHUAN-STYLE TOFU)   33
    Substitute 1/2 to 3/4 cup finely chopped cooked pork for the beef.
STEAK IN RED-WINE-MUSHROOM-CREAM SAUCE   34
    Substitute 10 thin slices cooked pork for the steak.
CORNED BEEF CARBONARA   37
    Substitute 1/2 cup julienne strips cooked ham or pork for the corned
    beef.
MUSHROOM, CHIVE, AND BACON BREAD PUDDING   56
LAMB CURRY   97
    Substitute 2 cups bite-sized pieces cooked pork for the lamb.
OPEN-FACED LAMB SANDWICHES WITH HORSERADISH   99
    Substitute 1 cup thinly sliced cooked pork for the lamb.
SPINACH LINGUINE WITH LAMB, LEEKS, AND ROASTED RED PEPPERS   106
    Substitute 1/2 to 3/4 cup cubed cooked ham, pork, or sausage for the lamb.
STIR-FRIED LAMB WITH FAVAS AND RED PEPPERS   107
    Substitute 1 1/2 to 2 cups julienne strips cooked pork, at room temper-
    ature, for the lamb.

7

POULTRY

MASTER RECIPES

LEFTOVER RECIPES

MASTER RECIPE:

ROAST CHICKEN

There are few dishes in the world as simple and delicious as a perfectly roasted chicken. This is a straightforward recipe that uses a variety of fresh herbs and a lemon to flavor the bird. It's so good cold that I often roast two birds at a time to make sure I'll have leftovers.

SERVES 4.

A 3-pound frying chicken, or a 3- to 5-pound roasting chicken
1 tablespoon vegetable or olive oil
1 lemon
About 4 tablespoons chopped fresh herbs, or 1½ tablespoons
  crumbled dried (tarragon, rosemary, basil, thyme, chives, and
  parsley)
Freshly ground black pepper
2 tablespoons butter, cut into small pieces

1. Preheat the oven to 425 degrees.
2. Rinse the chicken thoroughly and pat dry with paper towels.
3. Place the chicken in a lightly oiled roasting pan, breast side up. Score the lemon with a few *X*'s and place in the cavity of the chicken, along with half the herbs and a grinding of pepper. Rub the butter over the skin and wings of the chicken and sprinkle with the remaining herbs.
4. Roast the bird for 15 minutes, allowing it to brown. Baste the bird with the butter and reduce the oven temperature to 350 degrees. Roast about 1 hour to 1 hour and 15 minutes, depending on the size of the bird. To test for doneness, prick the thickest part of the drumstick with a fork; its juices should run clear yellow, not pink.

MASTER RECIPE:

CINZANO-GLAZED CHICKEN
WITH GARLIC AND CHIVES

I first tasted this outrageously good dish while visiting my friend Edwin Child in the south of France. We roasted a fresh bird with a whole head of garlic, a generous splash of Cinzano, and a sprinkling of garden-fresh chives. The slightly bitter flavor of the Cinzano mingles with the bird's natural juices and produces a thick, slightly sweet glaze. The garlic head is placed alongside the chicken, and is coated with the Cinzano and poultry juices, mellowing as it roasts.

This recipe also works beautifully with capon, Cornish game hen, and duck. Cook according to the size of the bird.

The chicken should marinate for several hours or overnight, so plan your time accordingly.

SERVES 4.

A 3-pound chicken
Salt
Freshly ground black pepper
5 cloves garlic, peeled
1 head garlic, unpeeled
Olive oil
1½ cups red Cinzano or sweet vermouth
8 chives, cut into 2-inch pieces

1. Place the chicken in a roasting pan and sprinkle the cavity and the skin lightly with salt and pepper. Place the 5 cloves of peeled garlic in the cavity of the bird. Rub the whole head of garlic liberally with olive oil and place alongside the chicken. Pour the Cinzano over the bird and sprinkle liberally with pepper and the chives. Marinate the chicken in the refrigerator for at least 1 hour (a whole day or overnight is not too long), basting occasionally.

2. Preheat the oven to 425 degrees.

3. Roast the chicken for 15 minutes. Baste the bird, reduce the heat to 325 degrees, and roast until the juices run clear when the inside of the thigh is pierced with a fork, about 1 hour to 1 hour and 15 minutes, depending on the size of the bird. Check and baste the bird frequently; if the pan juices dry up at any point, tip the bird slightly to remove the juices in the cavity, or pour a little more Cinzano over the bird.

4. Serve the chicken topped with the pan juices. Cut the whole garlic into quarters and serve alongside the chicken.

BASIC BROILED CHICKEN

SERVES 4.

1 chicken, cut into pieces
1½ tablespoons light olive or vegetable oil
4 cloves garlic, minced
Juice of 1 large lemon
¼ cup white or red wine
Sprinkling of chopped sage, thyme, tarragon, rosemary, or basil
Freshly ground black pepper

1. Preheat the broiler.
2. Place the chicken in a lightly oiled broiler pan, skin side down, and drizzle with half the oil. Scatter half the garlic over the chicken and pour half the lemon juice and wine on top. Sprinkle with the herbs and pepper and place under the broiler. Broil for 10 minutes, flip the chicken, and add the remaining oil, garlic, lemon juice, wine, more herbs, and pepper to the skin side; broil an additional 15 minutes, or until the skin is crisp and the juices run yellow and not pink when the skin of a drumstick is pierced with a fork.

ROAST TURKEY WITH OYSTER-HERB STUFFING

Every year we raise a dozen turkeys and have them slaughtered the day before Thanksgiving. The roasted turkey, stuffed with a savory oyster-herb stuffing, is the centerpiece of our holiday table. (We make sure to keep the largest turkey for our table so we'll have plenty of leftovers.) But don't wait until Thanksgiving to serve this bird. It should be enjoyed year-round.

SERVES 10 TO 12.

A 12-pound turkey
1 medium onion, quartered
1 stalk celery, chopped
4 peppercorns
1 bay leaf
Salt
About 6 cups Oyster-Herb Stuffing (page 51)
1 stick butter
1½ tablespoons minced fresh thyme, or 2 teaspoons crumbled dried
1 tablespoon minced fresh sage, or 1½ teaspoons crumbled dried
1 tablespoon minced fresh basil, or 1½ teaspoons crumbled dried
5 to 10 cloves garlic, peeled and left whole
Paprika
Freshly ground black pepper
1 to 3 tablespoons flour

1. Remove the giblets from the inside of the bird and discard. The liver can be used in a pâté (page 215). Place the neck, heart, and gizzard in a medium saucepan along with the onion, celery, peppercorns, bay leaf, and salt. Cover completely with cold water. Bring to a boil over high heat, reduce the heat to moderately low, and simmer for at least 1 hour, and preferably the entire time the turkey is roasting. Add water as necessary.

2. Place the bird on a rack in a large, lightly oiled roasting pan. Just before roasting, stuff the bird loosely (most stuffing expands) and close the openings using small skewers, string, or needle and thread. Tie the drumsticks together using a small piece of string or thick thread.

3. Melt the butter in a large skillet over moderately low heat and add the herbs and garlic; let cook about 1 minute. Take the skillet off

the heat and let the herbs and garlic steep in the butter for about 5 minutes.

4. Preheat the oven to 450 degrees.

5. Drizzle almost all the butter over the bird and sprinkle generously with paprika and pepper. Place in the preheated oven for about 15 minutes, then reduce the heat to 350 degrees. Baste the bird every 20 to 30 minutes, adding more butter if necessary. How long the turkey roasts depends on how fresh it is. Freshly killed birds cook much faster than previously frozen ones. You can figure *about* 15 to 20 minutes a pound, or until the internal temperature of the bird reaches 180 to 185 degrees. When you prick the skin the juices should run clear, not pink. If you wiggle the drumsticks they should feel loose.

6. Transfer the bird to a carving platter.

7. To make the gravy, remove excess grease from the bottom of the pan, using a turkey baster or large spoon. In the roasting pan, slowly heat the remaining juices and fat while gradually whisking in 1 to 3 tablespoons of flour. Cook this mixture over medium heat and slowly add the turkey broth you've been simmering all day. Simmer until thickened and serve the gravy, boiling hot, on the side.

ROAST GOOSE WITH
NEW YEAR'S EVE STUFFING

It was New Year's Eve and we were feeling decadent. The day was over-cast, the skies spitting out a cross between freezing rain and snow. It seemed the perfect opportunity to cook something special.

"How about a goose?" I proposed. "Too much work," everyone else moaned. "What else are we going to do today?" I countered. Before we knew it we were salting the insides of the goose and busy creating the world's most wonderful stuffing—a rich, tart combination of wild rice, cran-berries, macadamia nuts, figs, raisins, and pears. (This stuffing can also be used for chicken, duck, or turkey, or simply placed in a casserole and baked for about 30 minutes.)

Truth be told, a goose is an awkward bird. It's got a funny shape and requires a laborious cooking method—the goose must be defatted and basted with boiling water every 15 minutes or so in order to remove its massive quantity of fat. But do give this recipe a try on a day when you have lots of time and patience and the need to experience some truly extraordinary tastes and textures.

SERVES 6.

The Stuffing:
1 cup wild rice
1 cup cranberries
1/3 cup orange juice
2 tablespoons butter
1 large onion, chopped
1 1/2 tablespoons chopped fresh thyme, or 1 teaspoon crumbled dried
1/3 cup raisins
1 cup coarsely chopped macadamia nuts or pecans, almonds, or
   walnuts
1 cup peeled, cored, chopped ripe (or almost ripe) pear
1/2 cup chopped fresh or dried figs
1/2 cup chopped fresh parsley
Salt
Freshly ground black pepper

The Goose:

A 9-pound fresh goose, or frozen and totally thawed
1 medium onion, quartered
6 peppercorns
Salt

The Sauce:

1/4 cup dry sherry or port
Salt
Black pepper

1. Prepare the stuffing: Bring 2 1/2 cups water to a boil. Add the wild rice and stir well. Reduce the heat to low, cover, and let cook about 30 to 40 minutes, or until tender. Drain thoroughly and add to a large mixing bowl.

2. Meanwhile, mix the cranberries and orange juice in a medium saucepan and bring to a boil. Reduce the heat and let simmer about 8 minutes, or until the cranberries begin to pop. Remove from the heat and set aside.

3. In a skillet, melt the butter over moderate heat. Sauté the onion for about 10 minutes, until soft but not brown. Sprinkle in the thyme and set aside.

4. Place the raisins in a small bowl, cover with boiling water, and let sit about 15 minutes. Drain and dry thoroughly. (This process plumps the raisins.)

5. Add the cranberries, sautéed onions, raisins, chopped nuts, pear, figs, parsley, and salt and pepper to the wild rice. Stir well. (The stuffing can be made several hours ahead and covered and refrigerated. Never stuff the goose until you're ready to roast it.)

6. Preheat the oven to 425 degrees.

7. Prepare the goose and goose stock: Put the gizzard, neck, and heart in a medium saucepan along with the onion, peppercorns, and salt. Cover with cold water. Bring to a boil, reduce the heat, and let simmer, partially covered, while the goose roasts, until you have a flavorful stock.

8. Pull out any loose fat from inside the goose. Reserve for making goose crackling, if you like; check a good French cookbook for a recipe. Lightly salt the cavity of the goose and add the stuffing. Sew or skewer the cavity closed. Prick the goose skin with a fork in several spots. Dry the goose thoroughly with paper towels. Place it, breast side up, on a rack or on an inverted baking sheet set inside a large roasting pan.

9. Bring a pot of water to a boil.

10. Brown the goose in the preheated oven for about 15 minutes. Reduce the heat to 350 degrees, turn the goose on its side, pour 3 tablespoons of boiling water over the goose, and continue roasting. Pour another 3 tablespoons of boiling water over the goose about every 15 minutes, and with a bulb baster remove any fat that's accumulated in the bottom of the pan. After about 40 minutes, turn the goose on its other side and roast for 40 minutes more. Continue pouring hot water over the goose. Turn the goose onto its back and roast 15 minutes. Turn the goose over, breast side up, and continue roasting until the drumsticks wiggle easily and the juices run a pale yellow. The goose should cook a total of 2 to 2½ hours, depending on how fresh it is. Take the goose from the oven and remove the string or skewer. Let sit while you prepare the gravy.

11. To make the sauce, remove any excess fat from the bottom of the pan. Strain the simmering stock into the pan and bring to a boil over high heat, scraping up any bits and pieces from the bottom of the pan. Add the dry sherry or port, salt, and a grinding of pepper and let boil until slightly reduced. Serve with the goose.

ROAST DUCK

There is a myth about duck, that you must be a master chef to cook it properly. The truth is, duck is as simple to cook as chicken—it just takes a bit longer. This is a very simple recipe in which the duck is flavored with orange, herbs, and a small chunk of fresh ginger. Duck adapts to all sorts of interesting flavors—you could easily glaze your bird with honey and soy sauce, or fresh cranberry sauce, or cassis and orange slices, or with Cinzano and garlic cloves.

Because duck is such a treat and there is often no leftover meat, I usually roast two at a time (it's no more work than roasting one). That way I can serve one right away and save the other for superb leftover dishes. As many Chinese and French dishes demonstrate, previously cooked duck is a particularly tasty ingredient.

SERVES 2 TO 4.

A 5- to 6-pound duck, thawed if frozen, rinsed and patted dry
A 2-inch-square chunk of fresh ginger, peeled and left whole
1 small orange or lemon, scored in several spots with a sharp knife
About 1½ tablespoons minced fresh thyme, or 1½ teaspoons
    crumbled dried
Freshly ground black pepper

1. Preheat the oven to 375 degrees.
2. Trim any excess fat from the duck and place it on a rack set in a large roasting pan. Add about 1 cup of cold water to the pan to keep from burning the fat that will drip down while the duck is roasting. Using a sharp fork or knife, prick the skin of the duck in several places. This will allow the fat to be released while the duck is roasting. Season the cavity with the ginger, orange, half the thyme, and a generous grinding of fresh pepper. Sprinkle the remaining thyme all over the skin of the duck and season with pepper.
3. Place the duck in the oven and roast for 15 minutes. Reduce the oven temperature to 325 degrees and roast about 2 hours, or until the wings feel loose when jiggled. Baste frequently and tip the duck to remove any fat that collects in the cavity.

MASTER RECIPE:

POULE AU POT
(Boiled Chicken)

This is the proverbial chicken in a pot that mother makes to cure what ails you. And, truth be known, it works. But don't wait until you're sick to make this thoroughly pleasing, simple chicken dish. Not only do you get a perfectly tender chicken, and vegetables, but you're also left with a pot full of rich, flavorful chicken broth.

The chicken is delicious served hot, or can be used cold in salads, casseroles, and other soups. If you save the broth for another day, let it sit overnight in the refrigerator. The following day, skim off any fat and boil before using. The stock also freezes well.

SERVES 4; MAKES ABOUT 8 CUPS OF STOCK.

> 1 large chicken, left whole
> 2 carrots, chopped into large pieces
> 3 stalks celery, chopped into large pieces
> 3 medium onions, peeled
> 1 medium leek, thinly sliced (optional)
> 6 peppercorns
> 2 bay leaves
> Handful of chopped fresh parsley
> Salt

1. Place the chicken, vegetables, and seasonings in a large stockpot and add enough cold water to just cover the chicken. Bring to a boil. Reduce the heat and let simmer, partially covered, for several hours, skimming off any foam that accumulates on top. The chicken is tender when the legs feel loose. Taste for seasoning.

2. Remove the chicken to a serving plate and surround with the cooked vegetables.

TURKEY OR CHICKEN STOCK

MAKES ABOUT 8 CUPS.

1 turkey carcass, from a 12- to 20-pound bird, or bones and carcass
   from a cooked chicken, duck, or goose
3 medium onions, peeled and quartered
4 stalks celery, chopped
4 carrots, cut in half
6 sprigs of fresh parsley
3 bay leaves
8 peppercorns
Generous pinch of salt

1. Place all the ingredients in a large stockpot and add enough water to just cover the carcass. Bring to a boil over high heat, and skim off any foam that rises to the top.

2. Reduce to moderately low, cover the pot, and let simmer for about 2 hours, stirring occasionally to break up the bones and release flavor. Taste for seasoning and adjust as needed. Strain the stock and freeze or use as directed.

Greek-Style Turkey-Lemon-Rice Soup

SERVES 4.

4 cups turkey or chicken stock (page 193)
2 egg yolks
2 tablespoons heavy cream (optional)
Juice of 1 large lemon
Salt
Freshly ground white pepper
1 cup cooked white rice (page 123)
1 cup thinly sliced cooked turkey or chicken
Paper-thin slices of lemon
Minced fresh parsley

1. In a medium soup pot, bring the stock to a boil over high heat. Reduce the heat to low.

2. Meanwhile, in a small bowl whisk the egg yolks with the cream, lemon juice, salt, and pepper. Add 1 cup of the hot stock to the egg mixture and then slowly pour the egg mixture back into the soup pot. Add the rice, making sure to break up any clumps, and the cooked turkey or chicken. Heat until thickened, stirring, being careful not to let the soup boil.

3. Top each bowl of soup with a thin slice of lemon and a generous sprinkling of fresh parsley.

■■

Tortellini in Turkey Stock

This soup can be put together in just a few minutes. The turkey stock flavors the ring-shaped pasta.

SERVES 4.

1 quart turkey or chicken stock (page 193)
2 cups fresh tortellini, cheese- or meat-filled
½ cup julienne strips cooked turkey or chicken
Freshly grated Parmesan cheese
Finely minced fresh parsley

1. Bring the stock to a boil. Add the tortellini and simmer until tender (about 2 minutes if fresh and 6 minutes if frozen or dried). Add the turkey or chicken and let simmer a minute.
2. Pour the soup into bowls and top with a tablespoon of grated cheese and a sprinkle of parsley. Pass additional cheese on the side.

Spicy Chinese Chicken Soup
with Watercress and Bok Choy

This is a particularly hearty soup—a full meal, in fact—that should be served in oversized soup bowls. It's a staple dish of Chinese dumpling houses and luncheonettes.

The soup can be made with leftover chicken, pork, or duck. You can also use leftover cooked vegetables in place of the fresh cabbage and watercress. Thin strips of zucchini, carrots, celery, squash, and broccoli work well, as do crisp lettuce leaves.

SERVES 2.

4 cups chicken stock, preferably homemade (page 193)
6 ounces dried Chinese rice noodles
1 large leaf bok choy, or 2 small leaves from a Chinese cabbage, cut into 1-inch-wide strips
1 cup watercress, with the tough ends of the stems removed
Chinese chile paste
1 cup thinly sliced strips cooked chicken, duck, or pork, skin removed, at room temperature
2 tablespoons finely chopped fresh coriander or parsley
2 scallions, chopped
1½ teaspoons sesame oil

1. Bring a large pot of water to a boil over high heat.
2. In a separate pot, heat the chicken stock over moderate heat.
3. Boil the noodles in the water until tender, about 3 to 5 minutes, depending on the thickness of the pasta. Place a steamer tray over the boiling noodles and steam the bok choy and watercress for about 30 seconds, or until just limp. Drain the vegetables and set aside. Drain the noodles and set aside.
4. Place a small dollop of chile paste in each of 2 large soup bowls. Add the noodles, top with the meat and steamed vegetables, and pour the hot stock on top. Sprinkle with the coriander and scallions and drizzle the top lightly with the sesame oil.

■■
Thai Coconut and Chicken Soup

This traditional Thai-style soup is a luscious combination of sweet, sour, and spicy flavors. It can also be made with leftover cooked turkey, duck, beef, shrimp, or white fish.

SERVES 2 TO 4.

1½ cups coconut milk*
1 cup chicken stock, preferably homemade (page 193)
A 1½-inch piece of fresh ginger, peeled
4 scallions, sliced lengthwise and then cut into 1½-inch pieces
1 teaspoon chopped fresh lemon grass**
1 cup thinly sliced cooked chicken, skinned
¼ to ½ hot green chile pepper, seeded and chopped, depending on
   the degree of spiciness
Juice of 1 lime
3 tablespoons chopped fresh coriander

1. Place the coconut milk, stock, and ginger in a small soup pot and simmer over moderate heat about 5 to 10 minutes.
2. Add the scallions, lemon grass, chicken, and the ¼ chile pepper and simmer an additional 5 minutes. Taste the soup; if you can handle a hotter soup add more chile pepper. Remove the ginger and discard. (The soup can be made ahead up to this point.)
3. Stir in the lime juice and half the coriander and heat for about 30 seconds. Serve immediately, topping each soup bowl with the remaining coriander.

*Look for imported Thai canned coconut milk, available in gourmet and ethnic food stores. The American-made coconut milk sold in most grocery stores is loaded with preservatives and sugar.
**Lemon grass can be found fresh in Asian grocery stores or dried in gourmet and ethnic food shops. If unavailable, substitute 1 teaspoon chopped fresh coriander and ½ teaspoon grated lemon zest.

Sopa de Lima
(Mexican Lime and Tortilla Soup with Chicken)

I first tasted this cooling, soothing soup in Mérida, in Mexico's Yucatán region. I was immediately invigorated by the combination of spicy and sour flavors—chicken stock, fresh lime juice, tomatoes, avocado, sweet green peppers, hot chile peppers, and bits of crunchy corn tortillas. It quickly became one of my favorite soups.

If you have some leftover chicken stock and chicken meat, the soup takes only minutes to make. Serve it as a prelude to grilled chicken or steak, accompanied by warm tortillas and bowls of chopped onion, tomato, lettuce, and spicy salsa. Don't forget ice-cold Mexican beer.

SERVES 4 TO 8.

2 teaspoons vegetable oil
2 medium onions, finely chopped
1 medium tomato, chopped
$\frac{1}{2}$ large green bell pepper, seeded and chopped
About $\frac{1}{2}$ jalapeño or serrano chile, thinly sliced with seeds
3 limes
8 cups chicken stock (page 193)
2 cups shredded cooked chicken
Salt
1 large ripe avocado, peeled and chopped
Large bowl of tortilla chips
1 lime, thinly sliced

1. In a large soup pot heat the oil over moderate heat. Add the onions and sauté about 3 to 4 minutes, or until soft. Add the tomato and green pepper and sauté another 2 minutes. Add the chile pepper with its seeds, the juice of 2 limes and the shell from one of the limes, and the chicken stock. Let simmer 2 minutes and remove the lime shells. Taste the soup for seasoning. It should have a distinct lime flavor without being overly sour or pungent; add the juice of another lime if necessary. The soup should have a spicy bite, but shouldn't taste completely of chile; add chile pepper to taste. Add the cooked chicken and simmer until thoroughly warmed through. Season to taste with salt.

2. Meanwhile, place about 2 tablespoons of avocado into each soup bowl, along with a small handful of tortilla chips. Ladle the piping-hot soup into the bowl and garnish with a thin slice of fresh lime.

Chicken Salad with Curried Walnuts, Oranges, and Scallions

This salad can be made ahead and assembled just before serving. Serve with a warm loaf of bread and a platter of avocado slices sprinkled with lemon juice and olive oil.

SERVES 6.

The Salad:
About ³/₄ to 1 cup mayonnaise, preferably homemade
1 tablespoon curry powder
2 tablespoons chopped crystallized ginger, or 1 tablespoon minced
   fresh ginger
4 cups thinly sliced cooked chicken
2 stalks celery, chopped
2 scallions, chopped
2¹/₂ tablespoons drained capers
Salt
Freshly ground black pepper

The Curried Walnuts:
1 tablespoon butter
1 tablespoon walnut or vegetable oil
1 tablespoon curry powder
1 cup walnut halves

The Garnish:
1 large orange, peeled and thinly sliced
4 scallions, sliced lengthwise and cut into 3-inch strips

1. Assemble the salad: In a large bowl, mix ³/₄ cup of the mayonnaise, curry powder, and ginger. Gently stir in the chicken, celery, scallions, and capers. Add another ¹/₄ cup of mayonnaise to thoroughly moisten and coat all the meat, if needed. Taste for seasoning and add salt and pepper as needed. Refrigerate until you are ready to put the salad together.
2. Make the curried walnuts: In a medium skillet, heat the butter and oil over moderately low heat. Add the curry powder and sauté

about 1 minute; add the nuts and sauté for about 2 minutes, stirring constantly so the nuts don't burn. Drain the nuts on paper towels.

3. To assemble, mound the chicken salad in the center of a large serving plate. Place a line of curried walnuts over the top and surround with the orange slices and scallion strips.

■■

Turkey Salad with Grapes, Raisins, and Almonds in a Chutney Mayonnaise

SERVES 4.

The Mayonnaise:
¹/₃ cup plus 1 tablespoon mayonnaise
3 tablespoons chopped mango chutney
2 tablespoons fresh lemon juice
1 teaspoon snipped fresh chives

The Salad:
3 cups bite-sized or thinly sliced cooked turkey or chicken
3 tablespoons raisins or currants
1 cup red or green seedless grapes, cut in half
1 tablespoon butter
¹/₃ cup slivered almonds
Assorted greens (watercress, red leaf lettuce, etc.)
1 ripe avocado, peeled and thinly sliced (optional)

1. Prepare the mayonnaise: In a small bowl, mix the mayonnaise, chutney, lemon juice, and chives.

2. Prepare the salad: In a large bowl, mix the turkey, currants, and grapes. Gently fold in the mayonnaise.

3. In a small skillet over moderate heat, melt the butter. Sauté the almonds until lightly golden, about 4 minutes, stirring often so they don't burn, and drain on paper towels. Toss the almonds into the turkey salad.

4. Place the greens on a serving plate. Put the turkey salad in the center and fan the avocado slices around it.

■■

Florida Duck Salad
with Avocado-Grapefruit Mayonnaise

On a recent trip to the west coast of Florida I had a wonderful roast duck dinner. The portion was enormous and I was left with a good deal of duck meat. The next day, at a fresh produce stand, I bought some sun-ripened tomatoes, juicy Florida grapefruit, avocados, and Georgia pecans and put together this salad.

When I described the salad to a friend she said, "That sounds too wild for me," but then she tasted it and quickly changed her tune. Cooked shrimp is also delicious in this salad (page 67).

This is a perfect main course salad for a hot summer day.

SERVES 2 TO 4.

The Mayonnaise:

1 cup mayonnaise
1 very ripe avocado, peeled and pitted
3 tablespoons freshly squeezed grapefruit juice
Dash Tabasco or other liquid hot pepper sauce

The Salad:

1 cup thinly sliced cooked duck or goose, at room temperature
²/₃ cup thinly sliced peeled grapefruit
²/₃ cup pecan halves
1 medium ripe tomato, cubed, or 5 large cherry tomatoes, quartered
1 tablespoon walnut or olive oil
2 tablespoons freshly squeezed grapefruit juice
Salt
Freshly ground black pepper
2 cups assorted salad greens

1. Prepare the mayonnaise: In the container of a blender or food processor, blend the mayonnaise, avocado, and grapefruit juice. Season to taste with the Tabasco and set aside.

2. Prepare the salad: Mix the duck, grapefruit, pecans, tomatoes, walnut oil, and grapefruit juice. Season to taste with salt and pepper.

3. Place the greens on a serving platter. Spoon the duck salad on top and nap with a few tablespoons of the mayonnaise. Serve the additional mayonnaise on the side.

■■■
Warm Lentil and Rosemary Salad with Duck

SERVES 2.

1 cup cooked lentils (page 254)
1 1/2 tablespoons chopped fresh rosemary, or 3/4 tablespoon crumbled
   dried
1 1/2 tablespoons walnut or olive oil
3/4 tablespoon red wine vinegar
1 scallion, thinly sliced
1/4 cup chopped walnuts or almonds
1/3 cup plus 2 tablespoons chopped fresh parsley
Salt
Freshly ground black pepper
About 2 cups sliced cooked duck, goose, chicken, or turkey, at room
   temperature*

1. The lentils should be warm for this salad. If you have made them
in advance, simply steam them over simmering water or lightly sauté
them in a touch of olive oil.

2. In a bowl, mix the lentils, rosemary, oil, vinegar, scallion, nuts,
and the 1/3 cup of parsley. Season to taste with salt and pepper.

3. Place the salad in the center of a serving plate and surround with
the duck. Sprinkle with the remaining parsley.

*Drumsticks and wings should be left whole, and breast and thigh meat should be thinly
cut on the diagonal.

Composed Salad of Duck, Oranges, and Red Onion with a Warm Honey-Sesame-Orange Sauce

This salad can also be made with leftover cooked goose, chicken, or turkey.

SERVES 2.

The Sauce:
¼ cup orange juice, preferably freshly squeezed
3 tablespoons sesame oil
2 tablespoons chopped red onion
4 teaspoons cider vinegar
2 teaspoons honey
½ teaspoon soy sauce or tamari
Freshly ground black pepper

The Salad:
About 1½ cups Belgian endive, cored and separated into leaves, or
   watercress, with tough stems removed
1 cup thinly sliced cooked duck, goose, or chicken, at room
   temperature
1 orange, peeled, seeded, and cut into thin rounds
¼ cup very thinly sliced red onion

1. Prepare the sauce: Place all the ingredients in a small pot and whisk to combine. Simmer over moderate heat until slightly thickened, about 3 to 6 minutes.
2. Assemble the salad: Place the endive spears or watercress leaves around the outside edge of a salad plate. Place the duck in the center of the plate and alternate slices of orange and onion around it. Pour the warm sauce over the duck and salad and serve with a warm loaf of peasant bread.

Pasta Salad with Broiled Chicken, Feta Cheese, and Tomatoes

I was invited to a potluck dinner and had no time to shop or make anything elaborate. I opened the refrigerator and found a quarter of a roast chicken, a hunk of feta cheese, a few cherry tomatoes, black olives, sun-dried tomatoes, and some fresh dill and basil. This salad works equally well with leftover turkey, duck, goose, shrimp, or fish. Be inventive.

This makes a wonderful dinner on a hot summer night or can be served for lunch with a mixed green salad and a loaf of warm Italian bread.

SERVES 4 TO 6.

  1 pound spinach rigatoni, shells, or pinwheels
  3 1/2 tablespoons olive oil
  2 tablespoons red wine vinegar
  1 cup crumbled feta cheese
  12 cherry tomatoes, quartered
  1 to 1 1/2 cups thinly sliced broiled chicken
  1/2 cup black olives, cut in half and pitted
  1/3 cup chopped sun-dried tomatoes (optional)
  1/3 cup chopped fresh dill
  1/4 cup chopped fresh basil, or 1/2 teaspoon crumbled dried
  1/4 cup chopped fresh parsley
  Salt
  Freshly ground black pepper

1. In a large pot of boiling water, cook the rigatoni until tender, about 12 minutes. Drain, run under cold water, and drain again.

2. Place the pasta on a large serving plate or in a bowl and mix with the oil and vinegar. Add the cheese, cherry tomatoes, chicken, olives, sun-dried tomatoes, dill, basil, parsley, salt, and pepper. Serve cold or at room temperature.

■■■

Chinese-Style Chicken Salad

Colorful and dramatic-looking, this salad takes only minutes to put together. You can make the salad even more elaborate by serving it on a bed of cold rice or cellophane noodles.

Serve with rice crackers or very thinly sliced French bread, or simply eat by scooping the salad up into the endive spears.

SERVES 2 TO 3.

1 tablespoon soy sauce
1 tablespoon olive oil
1 tablespoon Chinese rice wine, or dry sherry
$^1/_2$ tablespoon sesame oil
$^1/_2$ tablespoon red wine vinegar
2 scallions, thinly sliced
$2^1/_2$ tablespoons sliced bottled pimientos
$1^1/_2$ teaspoons minced fresh ginger
Salt
Freshly ground black pepper
2 cups thinly sliced roast, boiled, or broiled chicken or turkey
1 small head Belgian endive, separated into spears

1. Combine the soy sauce, olive oil, rice wine, sesame oil, vinegar, scallions, pimientos, ginger, salt, and pepper. Mix with the chicken and let sit at least 15 minutes and up to one hour.

2. Place the salad in the center of a serving plate and arrange the endive spears around it.

■■■

Thanksgiving in a Sandwich

This sandwich is a ritual on the day after Thanksgiving. Sometimes, if we've eaten our meal early enough, we start making these sandwiches around midnight on Thanksgiving night.

It is superb with homemade mayonnaise and cranberry sauce, but store-bought sauces work, too, particularly when it's late at night and you want a quick, easy sandwich.

MAKES 2 SANDWICHES.

4 slices brown or white bread
About 2 tablespoons mayonnaise
About 4 tablespoons cranberry sauce (page 233)
About 4 thick slices cooked turkey or chicken, at room temperature
Salt
Freshly ground black pepper
About ½ cup leftover stuffing (page 50)
A few lettuce leaves (iceberg is a classic with this sandwich)

1. Spread each slice of bread with about ½ tablespoon of mayonnaise. Spread 2 of the bread slices with 2 tablespoons each of the cranberry sauce. Place the turkey on the other two slices, sprinkle with salt and pepper, and top with the stuffing. Pile the lettuce on top and put the two pieces of bread together.

■■

Little Moose Pond Sandwiches

There we were, miles from the nearest store, at the end of an idyllically peaceful weekend, with a near-empty refrigerator and enormous appetites. The bread was a bit stale, the avocado slightly brown, the Brie was looking crusty, but the chicken tasted as good as it had the night we roasted it. Leftovers are meant for inventiveness and these Little Moose Pond Sandwiches are a true testament to that belief.

SERVES 2.

4 thick slices bread
1 tablespoon butter
$1/2$ cup thin-sliced cooked or smoked chicken or turkey
$1/2$ avocado, peeled and cut into thin slices
About $1/4$ pound Brie, cut into thin slices (with the rind)
$1/3$ cup sprouts, preferably spicy radish sprouts

1. Preheat the broiler.
2. Toast the bread on one side. Remove from the broiler and butter the other side of the bread. Add the chicken and avocado and top with the Brie. Place under the broiler and broil until the cheese is bubbling.
3. Remove from the broiler and top with the sprouts. Serve open-faced.

Cold Sesame-Chile Noodles with Turkey

This dish was inspired by one of my favorite Chinese dishes, cold noodles with sesame sauce. Moist, meaty bits of turkey or chicken add terrific flavor and texture to the noodles. This is a perfect dish for a light summer supper or luncheon.

SERVES 4.

The Sesame-Chile Sauce:
2 tablespoons tahini
1 tablespoon chunky peanut butter
1 tablespoon minced fresh ginger
1 teaspoon minced garlic
2 tablespoons light soy sauce
1 tablespoon Chinese rice wine or dry sherry
1 1/2 teaspoons Chinese chile oil
1 teaspoon sugar
1/2 teaspoon cayenne

The Noodles and Turkey:
3/4 pound linguine, spaghetti, or Chinese egg noodles
1 1/2 tablespoons sesame oil
2 cups thin julienne strips cooked turkey or chicken
1 small cucumber, peeled and thinly sliced
1/2 cup peanuts
1/2 cup thinly sliced scallions

1. Prepare the sauce: In a medium bowl, stir together the tahini, peanut butter, ginger, and garlic. Slowly add the soy sauce, rice wine, and 1 tablespoon water; stir until the sauce forms a smooth paste. Add the chile oil, sugar, and cayenne and mix well. Taste for seasoning; the sauce should have a hot, spicy bite. Add chile oil as needed. This can be done ahead and refrigerated until needed.

2. Bring a large pot of water to a boil. Boil the pasta until tender. Drain and place in a bowl of cold water until you are ready to use.

3. Assemble the salad: Toss the cool pasta with 1 tablespoon of the sesame oil to make sure none of the noodles stick together. Add the sesame-chile sauce, half the turkey, and half the cucumbers and toss well. Place the noodles on a serving platter and scatter the remaining turkey and cucumbers around the side. Sprinkle with peanuts and scallions and drizzle the remaining 1/2 tablespoon of sesame oil on top.

Turkey, Potato, and Chive Pancakes

This is a potato pancake with tiny cubes of cooked turkey and bits of fresh chives added. The pancakes cook in a matter of minutes and make a great first course, or light lunch or dinner dish. Cooked chicken can be substituted for the turkey.

These pancakes are delicious served with a simple Lemon-Chive-Pepper Butter. You could also serve them with plain melted butter, salsa (page 237), or even a homemade cranberry sauce (page 233).

MAKES ABOUT 8 PANCAKES.

The Pancakes:
  1 medium potato
  2 tablespoons minced onion
  2 tablespoons flour
  1 cup skinned and cubed cooked turkey, white and dark meat, or
    chicken
  3 eggs, beaten
  3 tablespoons snipped fresh chives
  Splash of Tabasco or other liquid hot pepper sauce
  Salt
  Freshly ground black pepper
  About 2 tablespoons olive or safflower oil
  About 1 tablespoon butter

The Lemon-Chive-Pepper Butter:
  4 tablespoons butter
  1 1/2 tablespoons fresh lemon juice
  1 1/2 tablespoons snipped fresh chives
  Dash of Tabasco or other liquid hot pepper sauce

1. Make the pancakes: Grate the potato into a large bowl and let sit about 10 minutes. Use a paper towel to blot up any excess liquid in the bottom of the bowl.

2. Add the onion and flour and mix well. Mix in the turkey, beaten eggs, chives, Tabasco, and salt and pepper to taste.

3. In a large skillet, heat 1 tablespoon of the oil and 1/2 tablespoon of the butter over moderate heat. When the oil is hot, add 2 tablespoons of the batter to the skillet, allowing room for the pancake to spread. Cook about 3 minutes, or until golden brown, and flip to the other side.

Using a spatula, push down lightly on the pancake and cook an additional minute, or until golden brown. Stir the batter every now and then to make sure the eggs stay incorporated. Keep pancakes warm in a low oven until all the batter is cooked. Use remaining oil and butter as needed.

4. Meanwhile, make the butter sauce: In a small pan melt the butter over moderately low heat. Add the lemon juice, chives, and Tabasco and heat until warm.

5. Serve 2 to 3 pancakes per person and drizzle with the lemon-chive-pepper butter.

■■
Turkey, Zucchini, and Gouda Open-Faced Omelette

SERVES 2.

4 eggs
Salt
Freshly ground black pepper
1 1/2 teaspoons chopped fresh tarragon, or 1 teaspoon crumbled dried
1 tablespoon olive oil
1 tablespoon butter
1 teaspoon turkey fat or drippings from the pan (optional)
2 shallots, finely chopped
1 cup cubed zucchini
1 cup thinly sliced cooked turkey, dark and white meat
1/2 cup grated Gouda cheese (Swiss, goat, or mild cheddar can be
   substituted)

1. In a small bowl, vigorously whisk the eggs with the salt, pepper, and tarragon.

2. Preheat the broiler.

3. In a medium skillet, heat the oil, butter, and optional turkey fat over moderate heat. Sauté the shallots for 1 minute. Add the zucchini and sauté another 3 minutes. Add the turkey pieces and sauté 1 minute. Add the whipped eggs and let cook about 30 seconds. Scatter the cheese evenly over the top of the eggs and place under the broiler for 2 to 4 minutes, or until the eggs have set.

Stir-Fried Duck and Vegetables in Ginger Crepes

This dish makes an extravagant first or main course.

SERVES 4; MAKES ABOUT 12 CREPES.

The Ginger Crepes:
1 large egg
$1/3$ cup milk
Pinch of salt
$1^1/2$ tablespoons safflower oil
1 cup flour
1 to $1^1/2$ teaspoons powdered ginger
About 1 teaspoon safflower oil

The Duck and Vegetables:
$1^1/2$ tablespoons peanut or safflower oil
2 teaspoons minced fresh ginger
$1^1/2$ cups 2-inch-long julienne strips carrots
$1^1/2$ cups 2-inch-long julienne strips zucchini or snow peas
$1^1/2$ cups 2-inch-long pieces scallions, cut in half lengthwise
6 tablespoons 2-inch-long julienne strips fresh ginger
1 tablespoon chopped fresh coriander (optional)
About 3 cups thinly sliced cooked duck, goose, turkey, or chicken

The Sauce:
3 cups duck or chicken stock (page 193)
$1^1/2$ teaspoons minced fresh ginger
$4^1/2$ tablespoons Chinese rice wine or dry sherry
3 tablespoons chopped fresh coriander or parsley
$4^1/2$ tablespoons butter
Fresh coriander sprigs for garnish

1. Prepare the crepes: Whisk the egg, milk, $1/3$ cup water, salt, and oil in a large bowl. Gradually blend in the flour and 1 teaspoon of the powdered ginger and stir just enough to form a smooth batter. Let stand in the refrigerator at least 1 hour and up to 2 hours.

2. Heat a tiny bit of safflower oil over high heat in a crepe pan or 6-inch skillet. Spoon 2 tablespoons of batter into a ladle and pour into the hot pan, rotating to create a thin layer. Cook about 30 seconds, lift the crepe carefully, and flip to the other side. Cook an additional 30 seconds.

Stack the crepes on a plate and set aside. (The first crepe or two never seems to come out well, so don't be discouraged. Taste the first crepe to see if you can detect a subtle ginger flavor; add ginger to the batter, if desired.) Keep warm in a low oven. Makes about 12 to 14 crepes.

3. Prepare the filling: In a wok or large skillet, heat the oil over high heat. Add the minced ginger and stir for about 10 seconds. Add the carrots and zucchini and cook 1½ minutes, stirring constantly. Add the scallions, julienned ginger, coriander, and duck; cook an additional minute. Remove the duck and vegetables to a plate. Cover and keep warm in a 200 degree oven.

4. To prepare the sauce, heat the wok or skillet over high heat. Add the chicken stock, ginger, and rice wine and bring to a boil. Boil for about 4 to 5 minutes, until reduced by half. Add the coriander and the butter, remove from the heat, and stir until all the butter is melted.

5. Place a crepe on a plate and place a small portion of the duck on top. Pour a few tablespoons of the sauce over the mixture and garnish with a sprig of fresh coriander. You can serve the crepe open, rolled, or folded. Repeat with the remaining crepes and duck mixture.

■■■

Gingered Pea Pods with Duck

This dish takes only minutes to make. Serve with rice.

SERVES 4.

> 1 tablespoon safflower oil
> 1½-inch piece fresh ginger, peeled and cut into 1½-inch-long
>   julienne strips
> 1 pound snow peas, ends trimmed
> 1 cup thinly sliced cooked duck, goose, chicken, or turkey
> 1 tablespoon butter
> 1 tablespoon soy sauce

1. Heat a large skillet or wok over moderately high heat. Add ½ tablespoon of the oil and sauté the ginger about 1 minute, or until it turns a light golden color. Remove with a slotted spoon and set aside.

2. Add the remaining ½ tablespoon of oil to the hot skillet. Add the peas and sauté about 3 minutes, stirring constantly. Toss the duck and reserved ginger into the skillet and sauté another 30 seconds. Place the peas and duck on a serving plate. Add the butter and soy sauce to the hot skillet and swirl around until thoroughly melted. Pour the hot sauce over the peas.

Turkey Pâté

This is an easy pâté to make and puts to good use the huge, flavorful liver you get with every turkey. Serve with buttered toast triangles or French bread slices, Dijon mustard, pickled onions, and cornichons or gherkins.

You can also make this recipe with chicken livers, or 2 duck livers and cooked duck meat.

SERVES 6; MAKES ABOUT 2 CUPS.

    1½ tablespoons butter
    1 turkey liver, cut in quarters, or 4 chicken livers, cut in half
    Salt
    Freshly ground black pepper
    ¼ cup Cognac
    1¼ cups ground cooked turkey*
    4 tablespoons butter, softened and cut into small pieces
    1 teaspoon Dijon mustard

1. In a small skillet, melt the butter over moderately high heat. Add the turkey liver and a generous pinch of salt and pepper. Sauté about 2 minutes on each side, or until brown on the outside and pink on the inside. (If you're using chicken livers, sauté 1½ minutes on each side.)

2. Add the Cognac to the hot skillet, remove from the heat, and carefully light with a match. Shake the skillet until the flame subsides.

3. Add the liver and Cognac to the container of a blender or food processor along with the ground turkey, butter, mustard, and additional salt and pepper. Blend until smooth. Taste for seasoning and add salt or pepper if necessary. Place the pâté in an earthenware crock, 6 individual ramekins, or a medium serving bowl.

*Grind the turkey in a food processor or chop finely in a bowl.

■■

Turkey Tonnato
(Cold Sliced Turkey with Tuna Sauce)

This is my adaptation of the classic Italian dish vitello tonnato, in which cold slices of roast veal are coated with a tuna, anchovy, and caper sauce and served as a cold appetizer. I decided to try it using turkey (or chicken), and found that it works beautifully—the rich, pungent flavors of the sauce shine against the milder taste of the poultry. It's a great way to use leftovers from Thanksgiving.

Homemade mayonnaise is crucial to the taste of this dish. However, if you don't have the time, combine store-bought mayonnaise with 1 tablespoon of fresh lemon juice before using. Make this dish at least 8 hours before serving in order to give the turkey time to absorb the flavor of the tuna sauce.

SERVES 6.

The Tuna Sauce:
1 7-ounce can tuna, preferably Italian-style in olive oil, drained
1¼ cups olive oil
6 anchovy filets
2 tablespoons oil from anchovies
3 tablespoons drained tiny capers
Juice of 1 large lemon
Freshly ground black pepper
Salt, if necessary
¾ cup homemade mayonnaise

The Turkey and Garnishes:
12 to 14 thin slices roast turkey or roast or boiled chicken
6 anchovy filets
Capers
Bottled pimientos
Cornichons
Lemon wedges

1. Make the sauce: Place the tuna, olive oil, anchovies, anchovy oil, 1½ tablespoons of the capers, and the lemon juice in a blender or processor. Puree until smooth and creamy. Taste for seasoning and add pepper and salt if necessary (chances are you won't need to add salt

because the anchovies and capers are salty). Fold the remaining capers and mayonnaise into the sauce and taste again.

2. Assemble the salad: Spread a third of the sauce on the bottom of a serving plate and arrange half the turkey slices on top in a single layer. Cover the meat with another third of the sauce and place another layer of turkey on top. Spread the remaining sauce over all. Cover and refrigerate for at least 8 hours and preferably overnight.

3. Garnish the top of the dish with anchovies, capers, pimientos, and cornichons. Serve cold or at room temperature with lemon wedges on the side.

■■

Chicken Tortillas with Bean Salad

This recipe also works well with leftover steak, shrimp, lamb, or sausage.

SERVES 2 TO 4.

> **4 corn or wheat tortillas**
> **¹/₂ cup sour cream**
> **About 1¹/₂ cups thinly sliced broiled chicken or roast turkey at room**
>   **temperature**
> **1 cup Mexican Bean and Cilantro Salad (page 255)**
> **2 tablespoons minced fresh coriander (optional)**

1. Warm the tortillas in a low oven, about 1 minute on each side. Spread each tortilla with some sour cream and top with a few slices of chicken. Spoon the bean salad on top, roll up into a cigar shape, and sprinkle with coriander.

Duck Burritos with Chile-Cheese Sauce

Serve these burritos with a salad of avocado, tomato, and red onion, with a dish of salsa on the side.

SERVES 2.

The Chile-Cheese Sauce:
1¹/₂ tablespoons butter
1¹/₂ tablespoons flour
2 cups milk
About 2 tablespoons salsa, bottled or homemade (page 237)
¹/₃ cup shredded cheese (cheddar, Monterey Jack, or Swiss)

The Burritos:
1¹/₂ tablespoons olive or vegetable oil
1 medium onion, thinly sliced
1 tablespoon chopped fresh coriander or parsley
2 cups thinly sliced cooked duck, chicken, or turkey
4 medium wheat flour tortillas
4 tablespoons grated cheese (Monterey Jack or other fairly mild cheese)

1. Make the sauce: Melt the butter in a saucepan over moderate heat. Add the flour and stir to create a roux. Cook about 30 seconds, then slowly whisk in the milk. Allow the sauce to come to a boil, reduce the heat, and simmer about 5 minutes. Add about 2 tablespoons of salsa, depending on its hotness, and the cheese. Taste for seasoning and add salsa if needed. (The sauce should be fairly spicy; it won't taste nearly as hot once it's baked.)

2. Preheat the oven to 350 degrees.

3. Prepare the burrito filling: In a medium skillet, heat the oil over moderate heat. Sauté the onion for about 5 minutes, or until lightly golden but not brown. Add the coriander and duck and sauté another minute or two.

4. Place one quarter of the duck mixture onto each tortilla and sprinkle 1 tablespoon of the cheese on top. Roll the tortilla into a fat cigar shape and place seam side down in a shallow ovenproof casserole. Pour the sauce evenly over the tortillas and bake for about 25 minutes.

Chicken with Black-Bean-Tomato-Corn Sauce

Although you can substitute canned or dried ingredients, this dish is best in the summer or early fall, when ripe fresh tomatoes and corn are abundant. Serve with warm tortillas.

SERVES 2 TO 4.

¾ to 1 pound cooked chicken, turkey, or duck at room temperature
4 tablespoons olive oil
1 tablespoon minced fresh ginger, or 1½ teaspoons powdered
1⅓ cups diced fresh tomatoes, or 1 cup coarsely chopped canned
  tomatoes
1 teaspoon chopped fresh chile pepper
4 tablespoons Chinese fermented black beans, rinsed and left whole
½ cup fresh corn kernels, or ½ cup frozen or canned
Sour cream
2 tablespoons chopped fresh coriander (optional)

1. Cut the meat thinly on the diagonal and place on a serving plate, overlapping and fanning out the slices slightly. Set aside.

2. In a medium skillet, heat the olive oil over moderately low heat. Add the ginger and cook for about 30 seconds. Add the tomatoes, chile pepper, black beans, and corn and sauté 2 to 4 minutes, or until the tomatoes *just* begin to break down and the corn is slightly softened but still crunchy.

3. Spoon the hot sauce over the meat, top with a dollop of sour cream, and sprinkle with the chopped coriander.

Ellen and Roger's Vermont-Mex Turkey Casserole

A Vermont-Mex turkey casserole goes like this: tortilla chips are placed on the bottom of a casserole, and layered with leftover turkey, ripe tomatoes, grated cheese, chile peppers, and a mixture of fresh corn, coriander, and green pepper. Writers Ellen Lesser and Roger Weingarten created the recipe and serve it in their Vermont kitchen whenever there's any leftover turkey around.

This casserole is best made in the summer, when ripe, juicy tomatoes, fresh corn, peppers, and fresh coriander are available. But it's even good in the dead of winter using canned tomatoes and frozen or canned corn. You can substitute parsley for the coriander, but the dish won't have that distinctive Mexican flavor and bouquet.

SERVES 4.

1 1/2 cups fresh, frozen, or drained canned corn
1 cup seeded and diced green or red bell pepper
1/4 cup chopped fresh coriander or minced fresh parsley
Salt
Freshly ground black pepper
About 8 cups plain tortilla chips (not nacho- or cheese-flavored)
3 cups bite-sized pieces cooked turkey, smoked turkey, chicken, or
    smoked chicken
3 cups very ripe tomatoes, chopped in a bowl with their juice, or
    3 cups chopped canned tomatoes
2 cups grated cheddar or Monterey Jack cheese
1 small chile pepper, seeded and finely diced (optional)
Sour cream
Tabasco or other liquid hot pepper sauce

1. Preheat the oven to 350 degrees.
2. If using fresh or frozen corn, steam for about 1 to 2 minutes, or until cooked but still firm. If using canned corn, drain and set aside.
3. In a small bowl, mix the corn, pepper, and coriander. Season with a touch of salt and pepper and set aside.
4. Line the bottom of a large ovenproof casserole or baking dish with half the tortilla chips, overlapping them to completely cover the bottom of the casserole. Top the tortilla chips in this order: a layer of all the turkey, half the tomatoes, half the cheese, and half the chile pepper if using. Top with the remaining tortilla chips, the corn/pepper mixture, and the remaining tomatoes, cheese, and chiles.

5. Cover the casserole or baking dish and bake for 25 minutes. Remove the top and place the dish under the broiler for about 3 to 5 minutes, or until the cheese is bubbling and lightly browned. Cut and serve like lasagna, making sure each serving goes down to the bottom of the casserole. Serve with sour cream and Tabasco on the side.

■■■

Turkey with Wild-Mushroom-Tarragon-Cream Sauce

The rich, earthy flavors of wild mushrooms are the essence of this quick, simple sauce. Dried wild mushrooms are sautéed with fresh mushrooms and scallions and then reduced into a thick sauce with cream, turkey (or chicken) stock, and a splash of Cognac. You can add pieces of cooked turkey directly to the sauce (and serve over toast points or spoon into puff pastry shells), or pour the sauce over thin slices of turkey.

SERVES 2 TO 4.

$1/2$ **cup dried mushrooms (porcini, chanterelles, shiitake, or morels)**
1 tablespoon olive oil
1 teaspoon butter
1 cup sliced fresh mushrooms
4 scallions, cut in half lengthwise and into 2-inch pieces
$1 1/2$ tablespoons minced fresh tarragon, or $1 1/2$ teaspoons crumbled dried
Freshly ground black pepper
1 cup turkey or chicken stock (page 193)
$1/2$ cup heavy cream
2 tablespoons Cognac
Salt
8 thin slices cooked turkey or chicken

1. Place the dried mushrooms in a bowl and cover with 1 cup hot water. Let soak for 30 minutes. Drain the mushrooms, reserving the liquid. Thoroughly dry the mushrooms and slice them thinly.
2. In a large skillet, heat the olive oil and butter over moderate heat. Sauté the fresh mushrooms for about 3 minutes. Add the dried sliced mushrooms, scallions, tarragon, and a generous grinding of black

(continued)

pepper. Sauté about 2 minutes. Add the stock, cream, and $2/3$ cup of the reserved mushroom liquid. Bring to a boil, reduce the heat, and let simmer 5 minutes. Raise the heat to moderately high, add the Cognac, and reduce for another 3 to 4 minutes, or until slightly thickened. Taste for seasoning and add salt if necessary. Add turkey pieces and cook about 1 or 2 minutes, or until the turkey is warm, and serve over toast points or puff pastry shells. If you prefer to serve the sauce over thin slices of turkey, simply heat the turkey slices in a skillet with 1 tablespoon butter for about a minute on each side.

■■■

Chicken and Eggplant Curry with Coconut, Almonds, and Raisins

This is a particularly light curry. The eggplant is baked instead of fried so it doesn't soak up lots of oil, and the sauce is thickened with yogurt instead of cream. Crunchy bits of almonds, grated coconut, and raw scallions are added to the sauce just before serving, along with soft, plump raisins.

This curry works especially well with boiled or simmered chicken left over from a soup, stew, or stock.

Serve with white rice and bowls of condiments—mango or peach chutney, grated coconut, raisins, almond slivers, and chopped raw scallions.

SERVES 4.

1 large eggplant
1 1/2 tablespoons olive oil
1 large onion, thinly sliced
3 garlic cloves, chopped
1 tablespoon minced fresh ginger
1 1/2 tablespoons curry powder
1 tablespoon ground cumin
About 1/2 teaspoon cayenne
2 tablespoons flour
1/2 cup dry white wine
2 cups chicken stock (page 193)
4 cups bite-sized pieces cooked chicken
1 cup plain, low-fat yogurt

Tabasco or other liquid hot pepper sauce
1 tablespoon safflower or vegetable oil
¹/₂ cup slivered almonds
¹/₂ cup raisins
¹/₃ cup grated coconut
2 scallions, chopped
Condiments: mango chutney, additional chopped scallions, slivered
   almonds, raisins, and grated coconut

1. Preheat the oven to 350 degrees.
2. Cut the end off the eggplant and pierce in several spots with a sharp fork or knife. Wrap tightly in aluminum foil. Bake in the preheated oven for 35 to 45 minutes, or until just soft. Remove from the oven and let cool a bit. Peel the skin off and cut the eggplant into small cubes.
3. In a large casserole, heat the olive oil over moderately low heat. Sauté the onion, half the garlic, and all of the ginger for 10 minutes. Add the eggplant cubes and half each of the curry powder, cumin, and cayenne; sauté an additional 5 minutes, stirring constantly. Stir in the flour and cook a few minutes, until golden brown. Raise the heat to high and add the wine and then the stock, whisking. Let the sauce come to a boil. Reduce the heat to moderately low, add the chicken pieces and remaining garlic, and simmer, uncovered, about 5 minutes.
4. Using a spoon or a whisk, blend in the yogurt and remaining curry powder, cumin, and cayenne to make a smooth sauce. Let simmer for 5 minutes. Taste the sauce for seasoning, adding more curry powder or a splash of Tabasco if you like a spicier curry.
5. In a small skillet, heat the safflower oil over moderately low heat. Add the almonds and sauté about 3 to 5 minutes, stirring constantly to avoid burning, until the nuts turn a light golden brown. Drain on paper towels and set aside.
6. Just before serving, gently stir in the reserved almonds, raisins, coconut, and scallions. Serve with condiments.

The Very Best Chicken Pot Pie

Making a really good chicken pot pie is not difficult, but it does take time and a fair amount of care. What other explanation is there for the hundreds of mediocre concoctions that pass under the name of chicken pot pie? What is supposed to be a plentiful, cozy dish is often either too skimpy on the chicken and/or the vegetables, or dry and tasteless.

Modestly titled, this recipe combines a *generous* amount of chicken (or turkey), mixed with chunks of carrots, celery, mushrooms, and pearl onions in a creamy tarragon-laced sauce with pastry on the top and the bottom. It's best with fresh tarragon.

The entire dish can be put together ahead and baked at the last minute.

SERVES 4.

The Pastry:
2 1/2 cups flour
Pinch of salt
8 tablespoons (1 stick) butter
5 tablespoons lard or vegetable shortening
3 to 5 tablespoons ice-cold water

The Filling:
10 pearl onions, peeled and left whole
1 1/2 cups sliced carrot (1-inch slices, about 3 medium carrots)
3 stalks celery, cut into 1-inch slices
3 tablespoons butter
1 tablespoon olive oil
3 1/2 tablespoons flour
3 tablespoons minced fresh tarragon, or 1 1/2 tablespoons crumbled dried
3 tablespoons minced fresh parsley
1/3 cup white wine
2 1/2 cups chicken or turkey stock, preferably homemade (page 193)
1/2 cup heavy cream
1 1/2 cups thickly sliced mushrooms
2 cups sliced or chunks of boiled or roast chicken or turkey
Salt
Freshly ground black pepper

The Glaze:
   1 egg yolk
   1 teaspoon water

1. Make the pastry: Sift the flour with the salt into a large bowl. Cut the butter and lard into small pieces, and using two knives, work into the pastry until the mixture resembles bread crumbs. Make a well in the center and add only enough water so that the dough holds together. Knead the dough into a ball and place in the refrigerator for at least 30 minutes, or overnight.

2. Make the filling: Bring a pot of water to a boil. Parboil the onions for 6 minutes and the carrots and celery for 4 to 5 minutes, or until *almost* tender. Drain under cold water and set aside.

3. Preheat the oven to 425 degrees.

4. Remove the dough from the refrigerator and cut in half, making one piece slightly larger than the other. Roll out the larger half about one-eighth inch thick. Line the bottom and sides of a 2-quart Pyrex bowl or casserole, fluting the edges. Using a fork, prick the sides and bottom of the dough in several places. Place a sheet of wax paper over the dough and fill with 1 cup dry beans or rice. Place the bowl or casserole on a cookie sheet and prebake for 10 minutes, or until the dough begins to turn a golden brown. Remove from the oven, discard the paper and beans, and let cool slightly. Reduce the oven temperature to 400 degrees.

5. Meanwhile, roll out the remaining dough, place on a floured cookie (or baking) sheet, and refrigerate until ready to use.

6. In a large saucepan, melt the butter and oil over moderate heat. Stir in the flour to form a roux, and cook about a minute. Add half the herbs and the wine, whisking, and let simmer for a few seconds. Raise the heat to high and gradually add the chicken stock, whisking to create a smooth sauce. Let the sauce come to a rapid boil, reduce the heat, and add the cream. Let simmer for about 10 minutes, or until the sauce is thick enough to coat the back of a spoon. Stir in the mushrooms and cook about 2 minutes.

7. Fold in the parboiled vegetables, the chicken, the remaining herbs, and salt and pepper. Let simmer a few seconds and remove from the heat. Pour the chicken/vegetable mixture into the pastry-lined bowl or casserole.

8. Center the remaining dough over the pie. Flute the edges over the rim of the dish. If desired, use any remaining pastry to create a decorative shape for the top of the pie. (Use a sharp knife to cut out a chicken, leaf, tree, etc.)

9. Beat the egg yolk with the water in a small bowl. Brush the pastry with the glaze. Using a sharp knife, cut a few steam vents. The entire recipe can be prepared ahead up to this point and refrigerated for several hours.

10. Bake in the preheated oven 20 to 30 minutes, or until the pastry is golden brown.

■■

Moroccan-Style Chicken Stew

My friend Hanna Bulger spent two years living in Morocco while serving in the Peace Corps. She invited us to dinner one night and prepared Chicken Tagine, a traditional Moroccan dish of chicken stewed with onions, peppers, potatoes, and olives, all flavored by a rich cinnamon- and cumin-laced broth. We ate it the traditional way—out of a communal pot with large chunks of crusty peasant bread.

This is my adaptation of that delicious stew. Onions, carrots, peppers, and potatoes are simmered in a spicy broth, and then pieces of leftover chicken are added along with chick-peas and olives. You can serve this over a bed of couscous or rice. Or simply accompany it with a warm crusty loaf of bread and dig in.

SERVES 2 TO 4.

1½ tablespoons olive oil
1 large onion, thickly sliced
1½ teaspoons ground cumin
½ teaspoon ground cinnamon
1 heaping tablespoon flour
3 to 3½ cups chicken stock or 2 cups stock and 1 cup water
  (page 193)
1 bay leaf
2 potatoes, peeled and quartered
1 green bell pepper, seeded and thickly sliced
1 large carrot, thickly sliced
1 small dried red chile pepper, crumbled with seeds
Salt
Freshly ground black pepper
1½ tablespoons chopped fresh coriander
1 cup cooked chick-peas, drained
About 2 cups cooked chicken*
1 cup small black or green olives, with pits removed

1. In a large skillet, heat the oil over moderate heat. Add the onions and sauté about 5 minutes. Add the cumin, cinnamon, and flour and

*Keep wings or drumsticks whole and on the bone. Slice the breast and thigh meat into bite-sized pieces.

cook for a few seconds. Add 3 cups of the stock and the bay leaf and bring to a boil. Reduce the heat. Add the potatoes, peppers, and carrots and simmer, partially covered, until the potatoes are just tender, about 20 minutes.

2. Add the chile pepper, salt and pepper to taste, half the coriander, the chick-peas, and chicken wings or drumsticks and simmer an additional 10 to 15 minutes. If the sauce gets thick, add the remaining 1/2 cup of broth. Just before serving taste for seasoning; the broth should have a slightly spicy bite and the full flavors of cinnamon and cumin. Adjust if necessary. Stir in the olives and remaining chicken pieces and warm through. Sprinkle with the remaining coriander and serve.

SEE ALSO:

MEXICAN STEAK SANDWICH WITH AVOCADO CREAM   22
    Substitute 8 thin slices cooked chicken, turkey, or duck for the steak.
CELERY REMOULADE WITH JULIENNE OF ROAST BEEF
AND RED PEPPER   28
    Substitute 1 cup julienne strips cooked chicken or turkey for the beef.
STIR-FRIED STEAK WITH BROCCOLI, CASHEWS, AND SPICY
NUT SAUCE   30
    Substitute 8 thin slices cooked chicken or turkey for the steak.
JAPANESE-STYLE BEEF ROLLS WITH SCALLIONS   31
    Substitute 6 very thin slices cooked chicken or turkey for the beef.
MA PO DOFU (SPICY SICHUAN-STYLE TOFU)   33
    Substitute 1/2 to 3/4 cup very finely chopped turkey or chicken for the beef.
ROAST BEEF HASH   35
    Substitute olive oil for the beef drippings (and be sure to add any juices from the chicken), 2 cups shredded or cubed cooked chicken or turkey for the beef, and 1 tablespoon chopped fresh tarragon (or 1 teaspoon crumbled dried) for the sage.
SPICY CHINESE NOODLES WITH SHRIMP   79
    Substitute 3/4 cup chopped cooked chicken or turkey for the shrimp.
LAMB CURRY   97
    Substitute 2 cups bite-sized pieces cooked chicken, turkey, or duck for the lamb.
LAMEJUN (MIDDLE EASTERN-STYLE LAMB PIZZA)   101
    Substitute 1 cup chopped cooked chicken, turkey, or duck for the lamb.
SPINACH LINGUINE WITH LAMB, LEEKS, AND ROASTED
RED PEPPERS   106
    Substitute 1/2 to 3/4 cup cubed cooked duck for the lamb.

KEN HOM'S PASTA STIR-FRY   122
    Substitute 1 cup cubed cooked chicken or turkey for the ham.
CURRIED RICE WITH RAISINS AND SLIVERED ALMONDS   131
    Add ½ cup cubed cooked chicken, turkey, or duck and cook for 1
    minute with the rice.
FRIED RICE #2   132
SWEET POTATO AND HAM CROQUETTES   140
    Substitute ½ cup diced cooked turkey, duck, or goose for the ham.
STEPHEN'S SPICY SWEET POTATO AND CHICKEN   141
SAUSAGE, EGGPLANT, AND WHITE BEAN STEW   157
    Substitute 1½ cups thinly sliced chicken or duck for the sausage.
PORK IN A CAPER CREAM SAUCE   169
    Substitute 4 slices cooked turkey or chicken for the pork.
MEXICAN BEAN AND CILANTRO SALAD   255
    Add ½ cup cubed cooked chicken, turkey, duck, or goose.
PIZZA   264

8

SAUCES
and
CONDIMENTS

LEFTOVER RECIPES

OK, let's be up-front about this. It's a well-known fact that one of the most satisfying (and quick) ways to deal with leftovers is to simply open the refrigerator and eat. But a piece of grilled lamb tastes so much better when it's dipped in a Moroccan Hot Sauce, or a slice of cold turkey when it's smothered with Cranberry-Orange-Ginger Sauce.

In that spirit, this chapter presents a collection of traditional, and unusual, sauces and condiments to accompany all the cooked, leftover foods lurking in your refrigerator.

■■

Cranberry-Orange-Ginger Sauce

This is an updated version of the cranberry sauce recipe that originally appeared in my first book, *Condiments* (G. P. Putnam's Sons, 1984). Make this sauce in the fall when cranberries are fresh and plentiful and freeze it in small batches. Serve with leftover turkey, ham, or duck, or spoon it over pureed potatoes or squash. It's also excellent drizzled over a thick slice of pound, banana, or zucchini cake and topped with ice cream or whipped cream.

MAKES ABOUT 5 CUPS.

1 cup plus 4 tablespoons white sugar
4 cups fresh cranberries
$1/3$ cup orange juice, preferably freshly squeezed
$1/4$ cup maple syrup
$1/2$ tablespoon grated orange zest
1 tablespoon julienne strips orange zest
$1 1/2$ tablespoons coarsely chopped candied ginger, or $1 1/2$ teaspoons grated fresh

1. Mix the sugar and 2 cups water in a large saucepan and simmer over moderately high heat for about 5 minutes, or until the liquid just starts to become syrupy. Add the cranberries and simmer another 5 minutes, or until the berries begin to pop. Add the orange juice, maple syrup, grated orange zest, orange zest strips, and ginger and simmer another 2 to 3 minutes.

2. Pour the sauce into hot sterilized jars and store in the refrigerator or freezer.

■■■

Ginger-Cheese Sauce

This sauce is delicious on assorted cooked vegetables or poured over cooked pasta and baked until hot and bubbling.

MAKES ABOUT 1 CUP.

> 1 1/2 tablespoons butter
> 1 1/2 tablespoons minced fresh ginger, or 1 1/2 teaspoons powdered
> 1 1/2 tablespoons flour
> 1 cup milk
> 1/2 cup grated cheddar cheese
> Salt
> Freshly ground black pepper

1. In a medium saucepan, melt the butter over moderate heat. Add the fresh ginger (powdered ginger will be added later) and cook about 1 minute. Add the flour and stir to create a smooth paste. Cook about 30 seconds, or until the roux turns a light golden color.

2. If using powdered ginger, stir in the roux and then gradually add the milk, whisking to create a smooth sauce. Let the sauce come to a boil, reduce the heat, and add the cheese. Let simmer about 5 minutes, or until thickened. Season to taste.

■■

Ginger-Tahini-Yogurt Sauce

This sesame-and-ginger-flavored sauce perks up leftover cooked vegetables. It's also good with grilled fish, meat, or poultry, or spread on toast. Thinned out with an additional tablespoon of yogurt, it can be used as a salad dressing.

The sauce will keep in the refrigerator, covered, for several days.

MAKES A LITTLE OVER 2/3 CUP.

1 tablespoon minced fresh ginger

2 1/2 tablespoons tahini

2 tablespoons fresh lemon juice

1 tablespoon light soy sauce or tamari

1 tablespoon wine vinegar, sherry vinegar, or Chinese white rice
   vinegar

2 tablespoons safflower or vegetable oil

2 tablespoons plain, low-fat yogurt

1. In a medium bowl, mix the ginger and tahini. Add the lemon
juice, soy sauce, and vinegar, stirring to create a smooth sauce. Add the
oil and stir until smooth. Mix in the yogurt.

2. Let sit, covered and refrigerated, at least 30 minutes before using.
(If you want a thinner sauce, add another tablespoon of yogurt or milk.)

■■■■■■■■■■■■■■■■■■■■■■■■■■■■■■■■■■■■■

Green Sauce

This is a pungent vinaigrette seasoned with capers, cornichons, onion,
pimiento, and parsley. It's delicious with warm or cold slices of beef, lamb,
or poultry, as well as cold cooked shrimp or grilled fish.

MAKES ABOUT 1 1/2 CUPS.

1 cup olive oil

7 tablespoons white wine vinegar, or herb-flavored vinegar

1/2 cup finely chopped cornichons

5 tablespoons drained tiny capers

5 tablespoons chopped pimiento

4 1/2 tablespoons minced onion

4 tablespoons minced fresh parsley

Freshly ground black pepper

In a serving bowl, gently whisk all the ingredients together. Serve
within 2 hours at room temperature.

Moroccan Hot Sauce

This spicy, musky-flavored sauce is excellent with cold slices of cooked lamb or beef, or as a dip for cold cooked seafood or vegetables.

MAKES ½ CUP.

  ½ teaspoon cayenne
  1 teaspoon peanut oil
  2 garlic cloves, chopped
  1 small fresh chile pepper, stem removed
  1½ tablespoons chopped fresh coriander
  1 tablespoon ground cumin
  1½ teaspoons paprika
  1 teaspoon salt
  2 tablespoons red wine vinegar
  2½ tablespoons olive oil

  1. Mix the cayenne and peanut oil in a small bowl and let sit 30 minutes.
  2. Meanwhile, place the garlic, chile pepper, coriander, cumin, paprika, salt, vinegar, and 1½ tablespoons water in a blender or food processor and blend until smooth. Add the marinated cayenne oil and the olive oil a drop at a time until the sauce is smooth.
  3. Pour the sauce into a small saucepan and bring to a boil over high heat for 2 minutes. Remove from the heat and serve warm or refrigerate in a jar for about a week.

Oriental Dipping Sauce

This slightly spicy sauce is delicious with leftover grilled chicken, turkey, duck, beef, or pork. It can also be spooned over leftover rice or noodles.

MAKES ABOUT ½ CUP.

  6 tablespoons light soy sauce
  1½ tablespoons minced fresh ginger
  ¼ to ½ teaspoon thinly sliced fresh chile pepper
  1 tablespoon sesame oil

1. Mix all the ingredients in a small saucepan and heat over moderately low heat for about 5 minutes. Taste for seasoning; the sauce should have a bite.

2. If the sauce is too spicy, add soy sauce; if it's too weak, add an extra touch of chile pepper.

■■■

Salsa

(Mexican Hot Sauce)

This Mexican *salsa* is spiked with the distinctive flavor of fresh coriander. You can make it very, very spicy (as in oh-my-God-watch-out) or mild, depending on the amount of fresh jalapeño pepper you add.

Serve with leftover cooked chicken, turkey, duck, lamb, beef, even veal. It can also be used as a sauce for egg dishes or tortillas, and as a dipping sauce for taco chips.

MAKES ABOUT 2 CUPS.

> **2 large, very ripe tomatoes, chopped, or 2¹/₂ cups chopped canned tomatoes**
> **1 cup seeded and chopped green bell pepper**
> **2 scallions, thinly sliced, or ¹/₃ cup chopped onion**
> **1¹/₂ tablespoons chopped fresh coriander**
> **2 tablespoons fresh lime juice**
> **¹/₂ to 1¹/₂ chopped fresh jalapeño or serrano chiles**
> **1 tablespoon chopped garlic**
> **Salt**

1. In a large bowl mix the tomatoes, green pepper, scallions, coriander, and lime juice.

2. In a blender or processor, blend one-half of the chiles and the garlic. Add about ¹/₄ cup of water, and process until smooth. Stir the sauce into the tomato mixture, and add salt. Taste for seasoning, adding additional chile pepper if desired.

■■

Spicy Peanut Sauce

This thick, spicy sauce is excellent served with cooked pork, chicken, or beef. It also makes a good dip for cooked shrimp or raw vegetables, or a topping for cold Chinese noodles.

MAKES ABOUT 1 CUP.

> **1 cup chunky peanut butter**
> **2 thinly sliced fresh chile peppers, with seeds**
> **2 cloves garlic, minced**
> **1 tablespoon minced fresh ginger, or 1 teaspoon powdered**
> **1¹/₂ tablespoons sugar**
> **¹/₂ teaspoon cayenne**
> **4 tablespoons fresh lime juice**
> **4¹/₂ tablespoons light soy sauce**
> **2 tablespoon peanut or vegetable oil**
> **¹/₂ tablespoon sesame oil**

1. In a serving bowl, mix together the peanut butter, chiles, garlic, ginger, sugar, and cayenne. Stir in the lime juice, soy sauce, peanut and sesame oils, and about 4 tablespoons water, or enough to form a smooth sauce.
2. The sauce should be just thick enough to coat a spoon. Serve at room temperature.

■■

Tartar Sauce

Serve with leftover fish, fish cakes, or fried fish. The sauce will keep, covered and refrigerated, for several days.

MAKES ABOUT 1¹/₂ CUPS.

> **1 cup mayonnaise, preferably homemade**
> **1¹/₂ tablespoons tarragon or white wine vinegar**
> **¹/₂ tablespoon fresh lemon juice**
> **¹/₂ cup chopped cornichons or gherkins**

3 1/2 tablespoons minced onion
2 tablespoons drained capers
2 tablespoons minced fresh parsley
1 tablespoon snipped chives (optional)
1 teaspoon powdered mustard
Pinch of salt
Grinding of black pepper
1/8 teaspoon cayenne

In a medium bowl, mix the mayonnaise with the remaining ingredients. Refrigerate and serve cold.

■■

Quick Tomato Sauce

Use this sauce with leftover pasta, rice dishes, grilled meats, fish, or poultry, or spoon it over leftover stews and casseroles to wake up the flavors.

MAKES ABOUT 3 CUPS.

3 tablespoons olive oil
3 onions, chopped
1 28-ounce can Italian tomatoes, chopped, with liquid
1/2 cup dry red wine
2 1/2 tablespoons tomato paste
1/2 cup chopped fresh parsley
2 1/2 tablespoons crumbled fresh rosemary, basil, and/or thyme, or 2
    teaspoons crumbled dried
Salt
Freshly ground black pepper

1. Heat the oil in a skillet over moderate heat. Sauté the onions until soft, about 5 minutes. Add the tomatoes, red wine, tomato paste, parsley, herbs, salt, and pepper. Let simmer about 10 minutes, or until slightly thickened.
2. Puree the sauce in a blender or food processor. If you like a thick, chunky sauce you can use as is; if you prefer a thinner sauce, strain it through a food mill or thin-meshed strainer.

Yogurt, Cucumber, and Dill Sauce

Serve with leftover cold chicken, thinly sliced lamb, or beef. This sauce also complements a fish salad or can be served on or alongside leftover fish.

You can substitute chopped fresh mint leaves for the dill and serve as a refreshing counterpoint to spicy leftovers or curries.

MAKES ABOUT 1 CUP.

1 cup plain, low-fat yogurt
1 cup grated cucumber*
2 tablespoons finely chopped fresh dill
Freshly ground black pepper

1. Place the yogurt in a small serving bowl. Gently stir in the remaining ingredients and season to taste. Let sit at least 15 minutes before serving, but not longer than several hours.

*Peel a small cucumber and grate over a measuring cup.

SEE ALSO:

MEXICAN STEAK SANDWICH WITH AVOCADO CREAM   22
The avocado cream is also delicious with cold sliced cooked chicken, turkey, shrimp, poached salmon, or other firm-fleshed fish.
PORK, PEA, AND TOMATO SAUCE   171
QUICK ARTICHOKE AND VEGETABLE SAUCE   261

9

VEAL

MASTER RECIPE

MASTER RECIPE:

BRAISED VEAL WITH VEGETABLES

Try roasting a cut of veal the way you would a chicken or piece of beef, and you end up with a dried-out, disappointing roast. The reason is simple: veal has little or no natural fat covering it. Some cooks counter this by wrapping the meat in strips of bacon, but then you have an expensive roast that's overwhelmed by the assertive saltiness of the bacon.

My approach is a classic method: braising the meat in a covered casserole surrounded by a variety of vegetables. The result: an incredibly moist and savory piece of veal. You can use this braising method for all cuts of veal, except scalloppine and chops.

ONE POUND OF BONELESS MEAT WILL SERVE 2 TO 3 PEOPLE.

> **2 tablespoons butter**
> **2 tablespoons olive oil**
> **A 3- to 5-pound veal roast, boned and tied**
> **1 medium yellow onion or leek, thinly sliced**
> **1 large carrot, thinly sliced**
> **1 stalk celery, thinly sliced**
> **1 large clove garlic, thinly sliced**
> **¹/₃ cup minced parsley**
> **1 bay leaf**
> **Freshly ground pepper**
> **About ¹/₄ to ¹/₂ cup dry white or red wine, or veal or chicken stock**
> **1¹/₂ tablespoons balsamic vinegar**

1. Preheat the oven to 325 degrees.
2. In a large casserole with a cover, heat 1 tablespoon of the butter and 1 tablespoon of the oil over moderately high heat. Add the meat and brown on both sides. Remove the meat to a plate. Discard the fat and wipe out the casserole.
3. Add the remaining butter and oil to the casserole and heat over moderate heat. Add the onion (or leek), carrot, celery, and garlic and sauté about 10 minutes, or until soft but not brown.
4. Place the veal on top of the vegetables along with any juices that have accumulated on the plate. Add half the parsley, the bay leaf, and a generous grinding of pepper. Let the mixture come to a simmer, about 1 minute.
5. Cover the casserole and roast for 15 minutes. Remove and add ¹/₄ cup of the wine (or stock) along with the vinegar. Baste with any juices accumulated at the bottom of the casserole. Braise a total of 1 hour to

(continued)

1³/₄ hours, depending on the thickness and weight of the meat, or until tender when tested with a fork or sharp knife. Check the meat every 20 minutes or so, basting it with the juices. If the meat appears dry, add an additional ¹/₄ cup wine or stock.

6. Transfer the meat to a warm platter and remove the string.

7. Place the vegetables and juices in a strainer and press down on the vegetables to get as much pulp as possible. Skim off any fat and bring the sauce to a boil. If necessary, you can add an additional ¹/₄ cup stock or wine to stretch out the sauce. Boil about 2 to 4 minutes, and season to taste.

8. Thinly slice the meat on the diagonal and moisten with a few tablespoons of the sauce. Sprinkle with the remaining parsley and serve any additional sauce on the side.

Veal in a Piquant Green Sauce

In this recipe I wanted to combine the flavors of a veal piccata in a salad. Thin strips of cooked veal are topped with a piquant green sauce made from anchovies, parsley, capers, and lemon juice. Let the salad marinate at least 15 minutes before serving. Serve surrounded by steamed spinach, grilled zucchini, or endive spears and tomato wedges, and with warm slices of garlic toast or bruschetta (see page 48).

SERVES 2 TO 4.

1½ cups thinly sliced braised, sautéed, or roast veal, at room temperature
4 anchovies, cut into small pieces
3 teaspoons oil from the anchovies
4 tablespoons chopped fresh parsley
4 teaspoons drained capers
6 tablespoons fresh lemon juice
2 tablespoons olive oil
Freshly ground black pepper

1. Arrange the meat on a medium serving plate.
2. In a bowl, mix the anchovies, anchovy oil, parsley, and capers. Stir in the lemon juice, oil, and pepper.
3. Spoon the sauce over the veal and marinate about 15 minutes to 1 hour before serving.

Veal Salad with Asparagus and Olives

Serve this spring salad with a crusty loaf of Italian bread and a dry red wine.

SERVES 2.

The Salad:

1 cup julienne strips roast or braised veal
1 cup 2-inch pieces cooked asparagus
3 cups mixed greens (watercress, red leaf lettuce, radicchio, etc.)
$1/2$ cup small black or green olives, pits removed

The Sauce:

$1/4$ cup yogurt
$1/4$ cup mayonnaise
2 tablespoons minced fresh parsley
$1^1/2$ tablespoons fresh lemon juice
1 tablespoon chopped black olives
Salt
Freshly ground black pepper
Lemon slices for garnish

1. Assemble the salad: In a serving bowl or plate, toss the veal, asparagus, lettuce, and olives together.
2. Make the sauce: In a small bowl, stir together the yogurt, mayonnaise, parsley, lemon juice, chopped olives, salt, and pepper.
3. Garnish the salad with lemon slices and serve the sauce on the side.

Veal with Oranges and Tomatoes
on a Bed of Spinach
with an Orange Vinaigrette

This was inspired by a dish my friend Uri Stern made for me years ago. I re-created it in his memory.

SERVES 2 TO 4.

4 cups spinach, washed and dried, with the stems removed
1 cup cubed braised or roast veal, at room temperature
1 orange, peeled and cut into thin slices
1 ripe tomato, cut into small wedges
1½ tablespoons wine vinegar
1½ tablespoons orange juice, preferably freshly squeezed
4 tablespoons olive oil
1 teaspoon grated orange zest
Salt
Freshly ground black pepper
Sour cream

1. Steam the spinach until just tender. Drain thoroughly and chop fine.

2. Place the spinach on a serving plate. Arrange the veal, oranges, and tomatoes on the spinach.

3. In a small bowl, whisk the vinegar and orange juice and then the oil. Season with the orange zest, salt, and pepper. Pour the vinaigrette over the salad.

4. Serve at room temperature with a dollop of sour cream on top. Pass additional sour cream on the side.

Rotelle with Veal, Zucchini, and Red Peppers in a Parmesan-Cream Sauce

This is a particularly rich, delicious pasta dish. Use rotelle (known more popularly as wagon wheels or corkscrew) or any other medium shaped pasta.

SERVES 2 TO 3.

1 tablespoon olive oil
1 small onion, thinly sliced
2 garlic cloves, coarsely chopped
1 tablespoon chopped fresh rosemary, or 1 teaspoon crumbled dried
1 teaspoon chopped fresh thyme, or $1/4$ teaspoon crumbled dried
1 medium zucchini, cut into small balls using a melon scooper or cut into small wedges with a knife
1 small red bell pepper, seeded and cut into very thin strips
1 cup thin 2-inch-long slices braised, roast, or sautéed veal
2 tablespoons juices or sauce from braised veal (optional)
$1/2$ cup heavy cream
Salt
Freshly ground black pepper
$1/2$ pound rotelle
$1/3$ cup freshly grated Parmesan cheese
2 tablespoons minced fresh parsley

1. Bring a large pot of water to a boil.
2. In a medium skillet, heat the oil over moderate heat. Sauté the onion, half the garlic, and half the rosemary and thyme for about 5 minutes. Add the zucchini and red peppers and sauté 8 to 10 minutes, or until soft and almost tender. Reduce the heat to moderately low and add the veal, any juices from the roast, and the remaining garlic and herbs, and cook about 30 seconds, stirring thoroughly. Add the cream, salt, and pepper and let simmer about 5 to 8 minutes, or until slightly reduced and thickened.
3. Meanwhile, boil the pasta for about 10 minutes, or until just al dente. Drain and place on a serving plate or bowl. Add the sauce and cheese and toss. Sprinkle with the parsley and serve.

Veal-and-Spinach-Stuffed Mushrooms

You can also use this mixture to stuff 2 to 4 small zucchini (depending on just how small they are). Simply scoop out the inside flesh of the vegetable, keeping the zucchini shell intact, and spoon the stuffing inside. Bake for 15 to 20 minutes, or until the zucchini feel soft.

SERVES 3 TO 6.

> **About 5 to 6 slices cooked veal, any cut**
> **4 tablespoons freshly grated Parmesan cheese**
> **4 tablespoons bread crumbs (page 46)**
> **1 tablespoon chopped fresh rosemary, or 1½ teaspoons crumbled dried**
> **4 tablespoons chopped fresh parsley**
> **1½ cups cleaned, dried, shredded spinach**
> **1½ tablespoons butter**
> **½ tablespoon olive oil**
> **½ medium onion, finely chopped, about ½ cup**
> **12 medium mushrooms**
> **¼ cup heavy cream**

1. Grind the veal in a food processor or blender; set aside. (You can also finely chop the veal with a sharp knife.)

2. In a small bowl, mix the cheese, bread crumbs, half the rosemary, and 1 tablespoon of the parsley and set aside.

3. Steam the spinach over simmering water for about 1 minute, or until softened but not thoroughly cooked. Rinse under cold water to stop the cooking, drain thoroughly, and chop finely.

4. Preheat the oven to 350 degrees.

5. In a medium skillet, heat ½ tablespoon of the butter and the oil over moderately low heat. Sauté the onions and the remaining rosemary for about 5 minutes, or until soft but not brown. Add the spinach and cook an additional 3 minutes.

6. Meanwhile, remove the stems from the mushrooms and set aside. Place the whole mushroom caps in a very lightly oiled baking pan or ovenproof skillet.

7. Finely chop the mushroom stems and the remaining parsley, add with the ground veal to the skillet, and sauté 1 minute. Pour in the

(continued)

cream and heat another minute. Remove from the heat and stir in 2 tablespoons of the cheese/bread crumb mixture.

8. Spoon the mixture into the mushroom caps, pressing down lightly to get as much filling into each cap as possible. (The recipe can be made ahead up to this point, covered, and refrigerated for several hours until ready to bake.)

9. Sprinkle the remaining cheese/bread crumb mixture over the mushrooms and dot each one with a small piece of the remaining butter.

10. Bake for 15 minutes and serve immediately.

SEE ALSO:

OPEN-FACED ROAST BEEF SANDWICH WITH A SHALLOT-MUSTARD-CREAM SAUCE   21
Substitute about 6 slices cooked veal, with any fat removed, for the beef.

STEAK AND POTATO SALAD WITH HORSERADISH VINAIGRETTE   25
Substitute 8 thin slices cooked veal for the steak.

SPRING STEAK AND ASPARAGUS SALAD   26
Substitute 10 thin slices cooked veal for the beef.

CELERY REMOULADE WITH JULIENNE OF ROAST BEEF AND RED PEPPER   28
Substitute 1 cup julienne strips cooked veal for the beef.

MEDALLION OF BEEF SALAD WITH HORSERADISH SAUCE   28
Substitute about 10 thin slices cooked veal for the beef.

STEAK IN RED-WINE-MUSHROOM-CREAM SAUCE   34
Substitute about 10 thin slices cooked veal for the steak.

SWORDFISH SALAD WITH ROASTED PEPPERS AND ANCHOVY VINAIGRETTE   68
Substitute 1/2 pound thinly sliced cooked veal for the swordfish.

STIR-FRIED LAMB WITH FAVAS AND RED PEPPERS   107
Substitute 1 1/2 to 2 cups julienne strips cooked veal, at room temperature, for the lamb.

MUSHROOMS STUFFED WITH LAMB, PARSLEY, AND PINE NUTS   110
Substitute about 5 to 6 slices cooked veal for the lamb.

TURKEY TONNATO (COLD SLICED TURKEY WITH TUNA SAUCE)   216
Substitute 4 to 6 cups thinly sliced cooked veal for the turkey.

TURKEY WITH WILD-MUSHROOM-TARRAGON-CREAM SAUCE   221
Substitute 2 cups sliced cooked veal pieces or 8 thin slices cooked veal for the turkey.

10

VEGETABLES
and BEANS

MASTER RECIPES

LEFTOVER RECIPES

BEANS

This recipe is for dried beans simmered with onions, bay leaves, and peppercorns. The result is extremely succulent, tender beans that can be eaten as is or mixed in salads, stews, soups, and casseroles. These beans are much more flavorful, with a far better texture, than the canned variety.

I like to cook up a large pot of beans, keep some in the refrigerator, and freeze the rest.

SERVES 6 TO 8.

1 pound dried beans (pinto, red kidney, black, cannellini, or Jacob's Cattle)
2 bay leaves
1 onion, peeled and quartered
3 peppercorns
Salt

1. Place the beans in a large bowl or pot and cover completely with lots of cold water. Soak them for 12 hours. Drain and rinse under cold running water.

2. Place the beans in a large pot of cold water along with the remaining ingredients and bring to a boil over high heat. Reduce the heat and simmer, partially covered, for about 20 minutes to an hour, depending on the variety of bean. Taste frequently to make sure you don't overcook the beans. (One way to test is to scoop up a few beans in a spoon and blow on them. If the skin starts to peel off, the bean is done.)

3. Drain the beans, reserving the liquid, discard bay leaves, and serve. (The liquid the beans have cooked in makes a delicious base for a soup, stew, or casserole, so don't throw it out.)

MASTER RECIPE:

BOILED LENTILS

You can eat these lentils as is—hot, cold, or at room temperature—or use them as an ingredient in other recipes.

SERVES 4 TO 6.

1 1/2 cups lentils
1 bay leaf
4 peppercorns

1. Wash the lentils thoroughly. Place in a large saucepan and cover with 5 cups cold water. Add the bay leaf and peppercorns. Bring the water to a simmer and cook the lentils for about 20 to 40 minutes, or until tender. Drain and discard the bay leaf and peppercorns.
2. Use boiled lentils in soups, cold salads, or tossed with marinated cooked vegetables and a simple lemon vinaigrette.

MASTER RECIPE:

BOILED BEETS

Small beets are sweeter and more flavorful than ones the size of a baseball. Serve hot with butter, salt, pepper, and fresh dill, or marinate in olive oil, vinegar, and chopped onion to serve cold.

SERVES 4.

4 medium or small beets, tops removed
Salt
Freshly ground pepper
Butter
1 1/2 tablespoons fresh dill, chopped

1. Bring a medium pot of water to a rolling boil.
2. Scrub the beets clean and place in the boiling water for about 12 to 15 minutes, depending on the size, or until soft when pierced with a fork or sharp knife. Drain. Cut into thin slices and sprinkle with the salt and pepper, butter, and dill.

Mexican Bean and Cilantro Salad

Serve this salad with grilled meats and fish or add to a tortilla stuffed with chicken (page 217).

SERVES 4 TO 6.

4 cups cooked beans, preferably pinto or kidney
1 medium tomato, cubed
3 scallions, thinly sliced
¹/₄ cup finely chopped red or white onion
1¹/₂ tablespoons minced fresh coriander
6 tablespoons olive oil
3 tablespoons red wine vinegar
Tabasco or other liquid hot pepper sauce
Salt (optional)

1. In a medium bowl, mix the beans, tomato, scallions, onion, coriander, oil, and vinegar. Add the Tabasco and salt to taste, depending on how spicy and salty you want the salad.
2. Marinate at least 1 hour before serving.

Marinated Beets

SERVES 4.

5 tablespoons olive oil
2¹/₂ tablespoons red wine vinegar or balsamic vinegar
1 tablespoon minced fresh dill (optional)
Salt
Freshly ground black pepper
3 cups thinly sliced cooked, peeled beets
1 thinly sliced medium onion

1. In a medium serving bowl, whisk the oil, vinegar, optional dill, salt, and pepper. Gently mix in the beets and onion and taste for seasoning.
2. Let marinate for at least 30 minutes, or cover and refrigerate overnight. Serve cold or at room temperature.

Artichoke Heart and Avocado Vinaigrette

I adore artichokes and usually end up cooking too many. By the time I have eaten my way to the heart of the artichoke—the best part—I am too full to go on. Anyway, I've discovered that artichoke hearts taste equally good the next day.

For this recipe, you can use cooked artichoke hearts or the canned or marinated kind, but be sure to drain them well.

SERVES 2.

10 cherry tomatoes, cut in half
2 artichoke hearts, cubed
2 scallions, thinly sliced
$1/2$ ripe avocado, peeled and cubed
4 tablespoons olive oil
1 tablespoon wine vinegar
1 tablespoon fresh lemon juice
1 teaspoon Dijon mustard
Salt
Freshly ground black pepper

1. Mix all the ingredients in a small serving bowl.
2. Let sit for 15 minutes before serving at room temperature.

Pink Pancakes with Dill Butter

Each summer I grow an abundance of beets in my garden. Aside from boiling them and eating them plain, tossed with butter, I like to make salads, soups, and stews. One day I decided to experiment with some extra cooked beets, and the result was these delicious pink pancakes. Similar in flavor to Russian borscht, they make an excellent luncheon or brunch dish, or a first course for dinner.

SERVES 4; MAKES ABOUT 12 3-INCH PANCAKES.

The Pancakes:
$1^1/2$ cups flour
2 teaspoons double-acting baking powder

1 teaspoon salt
About 1¼ cups milk
2 eggs, at room temperature
3 tablespoons butter, melted
2 tablespoons minced fresh dill
3 cooked medium beets, peeled
About 1½ tablespoons melted butter

The Dill Butter:

8 tablespoons (1 stick) butter
3 tablespoons minced fresh dill

The Garnishes:

2 cooked medium beets, peeled and chopped
Sour cream
Lemon wedges

1. Make the pancakes: In a large bowl, sift the flour, baking powder, and salt twice. In a medium bowl, lightly whisk 1 cup of the milk with the eggs, 3 tablespoons melted butter, and dill. Gradually add the liquid to the flour mixture, stirring until incorporated.

2. Grate the 3 beets and gently fold into the pancake batter. Refrigerate the mixture for 2 to 4 hours.

3. Stir the batter gently. Thin it to pouring consistency with an additional ¼ cup milk if necessary.

4. Prepare the dill butter: Melt the butter over medium heat in a small saucepan. Stir in the dill and keep warm. (Prepare this just before you cook the pancakes.)

5. Heat a griddle or large, heavy skillet over medium-high heat. Brush lightly with melted butter. Ladle ¼ cup of the batter onto the hot griddle and cook until bubbles begin to appear on the surface of the pancake, about 3 minutes. Turn and cook until the pancake is golden brown and cooked through, about 1 to 2 minutes. Transfer to a heated platter. Repeat with the remaining batter, brushing the griddle occasionally with the melted butter.

6. Top each pancake with sour cream and sprinkle with some of the chopped beets. Drizzle with the dill butter and garnish with lemon wedges.

Spinach Feta Melt

This open-faced sandwich is a quick, simple version of a Greek spinach pie.

SERVES 1 TO 2.

2 thick slices bread
1 tablespoon butter or olive oil
¹/₂ cup cooked spinach, finely chopped
¹/₂ cup crumbled feta cheese*

1. Preheat the broiler.
2. Spread half the butter or olive oil on one side of the bread slices. Place under the broiler for about 1 minute, or until golden brown.
3. Spread the other side of the bread with the remaining butter or olive oil and the spinach. Sprinkle the feta evenly on top of the spinach and place under the broiler for about 2 minutes, or until the cheese is bubbling hot and the spinach is warmed through.

*A soft goat cheese or cream cheese can be substituted.

■■
Roasted Red Pepper and Vegetable Frittata

This is really a master recipe for a vegetable frittata. You can use any combination of cooked vegetable you'd like—trimmed green beans, florets of broccoli and cauliflower, slices of zucchini, pepper, carrots, celery, sweet potato.

SERVES 4.

> 1 large red bell pepper
> 2 tablespoons olive oil
> 1 small onion, thinly sliced
> 2¹/₂ cups bite-sized pieces cooked vegetables
> 8 eggs
> 1 tablespoon chopped fresh herbs, or 1 teaspoon crumbled dried
>   (tarragon, basil, thyme, marjoram, dill, etc.)
> Salt
> Freshly ground black pepper
> ³/₄ cup freshly grated Parmesan cheese

1. Preheat the broiler.
2. Cook the pepper under the broiler until charred and blackened all over, about 10 minutes. Wrap tightly in aluminum foil for about 3 minutes. Remove from the foil and peel, cut in half, remove seeds, and cut lengthwise into ¹/₄-inch-wide strips.
3. Preheat oven to 425 degrees.
4. In a large ovenproof skillet or shallow casserole, heat the oil over moderate heat. Sauté the onion for about 8 minutes, or until soft but not brown. Remove from the heat.
5. Arrange the cooked vegetables over the onions and place the pepper strips on top.
6. Lightly whisk the eggs with the herbs and salt and pepper to taste. Pour the eggs over the vegetables and sprinkle with the cheese. Bake until golden and puffy, about 20 minutes. When a toothpick is inserted in the center it should come out clean. Serve hot, warm, or at room temperature.

Cannellini (White Beans) with Garlic Sausage

This is a dish for garlic lovers. It makes a delicious accompaniment to roast or braised lamb, beef, or chicken, or it can be served on its own.

SERVES 2 TO 4.

1 1/2 tablespoons olive oil
1 cup thinly sliced onions
2 tablespoons thinly sliced garlic
1/4 cup dry white wine
2 cups cooked white beans (page 253)
1 cup thinly sliced cooked or raw sausage* (garlic, or hot or sweet Italian)
1 tablespoon chopped garlic
Freshly ground black pepper
2 1/2 tablespoons finely chopped fresh parsley

1. In a medium skillet, heat the oil over moderate heat. Sauté the onions and sliced garlic for about 10 minutes, or until soft but not brown. Add the wine and simmer for a minute.

2. Gently stir in the cooked beans, cooked sausage, chopped garlic, and pepper and cook for 10 minutes. Sprinkle with the chopped parsley.

*If using raw sausage, follow the Master Recipe on page 150.

■■

Quick Artichoke and Vegetable Sauce

This sauce can be made with virtually any leftover cooked vegetables. I made it one spring day when I found a cooked artichoke and a few asparagus spears left over in my refrigerator. If you want to substitute other vegetables, use a total of 1 cup cooked vegetables, cut into bite-sized pieces.

Serve over half a pound of linguine or fettuccine or with rice, bulgur, lentils, or couscous.

SERVES 1 TO 2.

3¹/₂ tablespoons olive oil
2 garlic cloves, chopped
1 cooked artichoke heart, cubed
¹/₂ cup bite-sized pieces cooked asparagus
2 tablespoons snipped fresh chives or minced fresh parsley
Freshly ground black pepper
Freshly grated Parmesan cheese

1. In a small skillet, heat 2 tablespoons of the oil over moderate heat. Sauté the garlic for about 2 minutes. Add the artichoke heart and asparagus and sauté about 2 minutes, or until warm and beginning to turn golden.

2. Add the chives and pepper and pour over pasta or other grain. Top with the remaining oil and toss with the cheese.

IDEAS FOR LEFTOVER VEGETABLES

➤Keep a jar of spicy marinade in the refrigerator and add leftover cooked vegetables to it. Make a mixture of vinegar, olive oil, a touch of dry wine, spices (basil, thyme, oregano, and tarragon), and peeled cloves of garlic. Let the vegetables sit in the marinade for about 24 hours, then serve with salads, cold meats, poultry, and fish, or as a cold antipasto platter. The marinade will stay fresh for up to a month; keep adding vegetables.

➤Add about 2 cups cooked assorted vegetables to 4 cups cooked pasta shells. Toss with lemon juice, olive oil, a cubed tomato, and chopped fresh basil and serve cold or at room temperature.

➤Make a vegetable pizza (pages 264, 265).

➤Make a Ginger-Cheese Sauce (page 234). Place 3 cups cooked vegetables in a lightly oiled casserole. Top with 1 cup of Ginger-Cheese Sauce, sprinkle lightly with bread crumbs (page 46), and bake 30 minutes, or until hot and bubbling.

➤Heat a tablespoon of oil in a wok. Add a tablespoon each of minced garlic and fresh ginger and sauté for a minute. Add a few cups of assorted cooked vegetables and stir-fry until hot. Top with soy sauce, tahini, sesame seeds, bits of sautéed ham, or chile sauce.

➤Serve a platter of cooked vegetables with a garlic-yogurt-basil dip. Place 1 cup yogurt or sour cream, 1 cup fresh basil leaves, 2 cloves garlic, and 1/2 cup pine nuts or walnuts in a blender or food processor and blend until smooth.

➤Make a veggie hero sandwich: Split a loaf of French bread lengthwise, sprinkle liberally with oil and vinegar, and layer it with slices of tomato, red onion, green or red pepper, pickled peppers, grated or thinly sliced cheese, and lots of cooked vegetables.

➤You've had a party. The crudités were a big hit, but you've still got a refrigerator full of leftovers. The vegetables are just starting to look a bit limp, but they are nowhere near extinction. Boil up some water and lightly steam the vegetables until tender. Serve with Oriental Dipping Sauce (page 236), Spicy Peanut Sauce (page 238), Moroccan Hot Sauce (page 236), Ginger-Tahini-Yogurt Sauce (page 234), or Green Sauce (page 235).

SEE ALSO:

Substitute 1/2 pound chopped cooked spinach, kale, peas, peppers, artichoke hearts, or broccoli for the asparagus.

Add 1/3 to 1/2 cup chopped cooked spinach or other vegetables.

Add 1/2 cup cooked peas or other chopped cooked vegetables.

Add 1/2 cup chopped cooked eggplant, carrots, or other vegetables.

Substitute 4 cups assorted cooked vegetables for the raw vegetables, or add 2 cups cooked vegetables and 2 cups raw. However, if you are using cooked vegetables instead of fresh, add them to the soup only for the last 5 minutes. You simply want to reheat them in the broth, without overcooking them. Don't use overcooked or very limp vegetables.

Add 1/2 to 1 cup assorted cooked vegetables instead of, or in addition to, the bacon.

Add 1 cup thin strips cooked vegetables instead of, or in addition to, the chicken.

PIZZA
—ANYTHING GOES FOR LEFTOVERS

Pizza is an ideal way to use leftovers. Think of the pizza dough as an artist's canvas and your leftovers as the paints and colors that create the painting. Anything goes with pizza; you can have fun mixing leftover vegetables with meats, fish, or poultry. If the combination sounds good to you, chances are it will be. Dare to be wild. Lamb, goat cheese, and rosemary; shrimp, mushrooms, chives, and fontina cheese; duck, sun-dried tomatoes, and smoked mozzarella; pesto, artichoke hearts, and chicken. Zucchini, tomatoes, olives, caramelized onions, thyme, and Parmesan; sausage, oregano, and eggplant.

MASTER RECIPE::

PIZZA

What follows is a master recipe for pizza crust, along with some basic suggestions for creating pizza toppings. It can be made ahead and frozen or refrigerated for several days.

A DEEP-DISH PIZZA SERVES 4; A THIN ONE, 2–3.

The Pizza Dough:
> 1 tablespoon active dry yeast
> 1 1/2 cups *warm* water
> About 3 to 3 1/2 cups unbleached flour
> 1/2 teaspoon salt
> 2 tablespoons olive oil
> About 2 tablespoons cornmeal, for dusting pizza sheet

1. Mix the yeast with the water in a large bowl and place in a warm spot for 5 minutes, or until the yeast begins to bubble and foam. (If the yeast does not foam, discard and begin again using fresh yeast.)

2. Sift 3 cups of the flour and the salt into the yeast and gradually mix to form a ball. Mix in the olive oil and enough additional flour to form a soft ball.

3. Transfer the dough to a lightly floured work surface and knead it until soft and elastic, about 10 minutes. Shape into a ball and place in a lightly oiled bowl, turning the dough to coat with the oil on all sides. Cover with a clean tea towel and place in a warm, draft-free spot for about 1 hour, or until the dough has doubled in bulk. Punch down the dough and reshape into a ball. Cover and let sit another 20 minutes, or until the dough rises again. Punch down again and divide the dough in half or quarters, depending on the size of the pizza you're making. (To freeze any remaining dough simply wrap in plastic; thaw before proceeding.) Set the dough in the refrigerator until the topping is ready.

4. Sprinkle a pizza sheet with the cornmeal. You can roll the dough out very thin or shape it into a thick deep-dish-style pizza. Spread a thin coating of olive oil on the dough, sprinkle with finely chopped garlic and herbs, and then add your other toppings.

5. Generally, you want to add about 1 1/2 cups meat or fish, 1 1/2 cups vegetables, and about 1 to 2 cups of cheese to make two 10- to 12-inch thin pizzas or 1 deep-dish pizza.

6. Bake the pizza in an oven preheated to 500 degrees for about 6 to 8 minutes for a thin pizza, or until the crust begins to turn a light golden brown. Deep-dish pizza takes about 20 to 25 minutes for the crust and filling to cook properly.

INDEX

Almonds
  and beef sandwiches, 19
  and bread and herb stuffed tomatoes, 55
  and chicken and eggplant curry, 222–23
  in chicken salad, 201
  curried rice with raisins and, 131
  in fish/lamb and rice stuffed zucchini, 81, 109
  and Italian bread salad, 54
  in lentil and rosemary salad with duck, 203
  in turkey salad, 201
Anchovy, 68, 161, 216–17, 245
Angel food cake, 45
Antipasto, 46, 49
Apple cider, 149, 150, 168–69
Apples, 23, 51, 162, 168–69
Artichokes, 118, 256, 261, 263, 264
Arugula, 19, 25, 160–61
Asparagus, 26, 75, 80–81, 93, 107, 118, 246, 261
Avocados, 22–23, 199, 201, 202, 208, 256

Bacon, 56–57, 120, 175–76
Baguette, ham, cheese and herb, 172–73
Baked ham, 149
Baked potatoes, 133, 138
Bananas, 45
Barley, 94
Bass, 74
Beans
  as a basic ingredient, 1–2
  and cilantro salad, 217, 255
  fava, 107
  and fish salad, 70–71
  green, 70–71, 163
  homemade, 154–55, 157
  liquid from, 253

Beans *(cont.)*
  master recipe for, 253
  Mediterranean-style tuna salad and, 39, 71
  mung, 130–31, 162
  and pasta soup with pork, 153
  and pork salad, 158
  and sausage and eggplant stew, 157
  and sausages, 151
  stir-fried with lamb and peppers, 107
  in succotash with ham, 163
  and tuna salad, 71
  See also Black beans; Cannellini beans
Beef
  with black bean, tomato and corn sauce, 39, 219
  boiled, 14–15, 35
  bones, 38
  brisket, 16, 35
  with cannellini beans, 260
  celery remoulade with julienne of roast, 28
  Chinese, 39, 95
  and Chinese noodles, 39, 76–77
  corned, 17, 24, 29, 35, 36, 37
  and curried rice with raisins and almonds, 39, 131
  curry, 39, 97
  and gingered pea pods, 40, 204
  in a green sauce, 40, 245
  hash, 35–36
  hot pot, 39, 95
  leftover recipes for, 19–40
  in ma po dofu, 33
  master recipes for, 13–18
  in moussaka, 39, 104–5
  parsley and pine nuts stuffed mushrooms, 39, 110–11

Linguine, 117, 209
Little Moose Pond sandwiches, 208
Lobster, 66–67, 72–73, 75, 78, 79, 80–81,
    106

Macaroni, 120
Mahi-mahi, 68
Maple butter, 165
Maple syrup, 52, 132, 134, 165, 233
Ma po dofu, 33
Marinade, for vegetables, 262
Mayonnaise
    apple and horseradish, 23
    avocado and grapefruit, 202
    as a basic ingredient, 2
    and beef sandwiches, 19
    and celery remoulade and roast beef, 27
    in chicken salad, 200–201
    chutney, 201
    curry-cumin, 19
    garlic-flavored, 19
    in potato salad, 138, 139
    in Russian dressing, 24
    for sauce for veal salad with asparagus
        and olives, 246
    and shrimp, pea and pasta salad, 69
    in tartar sauce, 238–39
    in Thanksgiving in a sandwich, 207
    in tuna sauce, 216–17
Meatballs, 117
Mediterranean-style tuna and bean salad,
    39, 71
Mexican bean and cilantro salad, 255
Mexican steak sandwich, 22–23
Middle Eastern-style lamb, 98–99, 101–3
Mint, 27, 86–87, 98–99, 158
Monterey Jack cheese, 136, 220–21
Moroccan hot sauce, 236
Moroccan-style chicken, 226–27
Moussaka, 104–5
Mozzarella cheese, 3, 19, 102–3, 175–76,
    264
Muenster cheese, 142
Mung beans, 162
Mushrooms
    as a basic ingredient, 5
    and bread, 48
    in chicken pot pie, 224–25
    Chinese, 95
    chive, and bacon bread pudding, 56–57
    creamed, 57
    in fried rice with chicken and peanuts,
        129
    in oriental rice salad, 128

Mushrooms *(cont.)*
    in pasta frittata, 119
    in pizza, 264
    risotto with dried, 124–25
    sautéed wild, 48
    and steak in red wine, mushroom and
        cream sauce, 34
    stuffed with lamb, parsley and pine nuts,
        110–11
    stuffed with lamb and spinach, 111
    stuffed with veal and spinach, 249–50
    and stuffing, 51
    tarragon and cream sauce, 221–22
Mussels, 72–73
Mustard
    as a basic ingredient, 2
    in celery remoulade and roast beef, 27
    in fish cakes, 74
    and lamb, 86–87
    peppercorn, 19
    in pork with a caper cream sauce, 169
    in potato salad, 138, 139
    and roast pork, 150
    and swordfish, 61
    in turkey pâté, 215
Mustard—in sauces
    apple, mustard and wine, 168–69
    shallots and cream, 21
    with soy sauce, 161
    steak in red wine, mushroom and cream
        sauce, 34
    tartar, 238–39
Mustard—in vinaigrette
    artichoke heart and avocado, 256
    horseradish, 25
    lemon, basil and parmesan cheese, 160–61
    mustard and soy sauce, 161
    parmesan cheese, 159

New Year's Eve stuffing, 188–90
Noodles
    and turkey, 209
    See also Chinese noodles; Pasta
Nuts, 19, 30, 45, 188–90
    as basic ingredients, 5
    See also name of specific type of nut

Oils, as basic ingredients, 5–6
Olives
    in chicken stew, 226–27
    and garlic, 49
    with lamb, tomatoes and lemon zest, 108
    in lamb sandwiches, 96
    in pizza, 264

Tamari, 7
Tartar sauce, 238–39
Tarts, 80–81, 164–65
Thai coconut and chicken soup, 198
Thanksgiving in a sandwich, 207
Tomatoes
  and bluefish, onions and basil, 63
  bread and herb stuffed, 55
  in chicken with black bean, tomato and
    corn sauce, 219
  and garlic bread, 48
  and lamb, 88–89, 90
  with lamb, olives and lemon zest,
    108
  in lamb pizza, 102–3
  in lamb stock, 90
  in pasta e fagioli, 153
  in pasta frittata, 119
  in pizza, 264
  and poached scallops, 66
  in Quiche Lorraine, 175–76
  in salsa, 22, 237
  in sandwiches, 19, 96, 98–99
  in sauces, 171, 219, 239
  in shepherdess pie, 100–101
  stir-fried with lamb and favas and
    peppers, 107
  in turkey casserole, 220–21
  in vegetables with pasta, 262
  in vinaigrette, 256
  See also Sun-dried tomatoes
Tomatoes—in salads
  duck, 202
  Italian bread, 54
  Mexican bean and cilantro, 255
  pasta with asparagus, feta cheese, tomato
    and dill salad, 118, 205
  pork and bean, 158
  veal, 247
Tomatoes—in soups/stews
  fish, 72–73
  lamb, lentil and rosemary, 91
  lamb, orzo and dill, 92
  lime and tortilla, 199
  sausage, eggplant and bean, 157
  vegetable with ham, 154–55
Tomato paste, 122, 169, 171, 239
Tomato sauce, 104–5, 109, 117, 119, 153,
  239
Tortellini, 196
Tortilla chips, 220–21
Tortillas, 111, 199, 217, 881
Tuna, 26, 39, 64, 68, 70, 72–73, 82
Tuna sauce, 216–17

Turkey
  burritos with chile-cheese sauce,
    218
  and celery remoulade with peppers, 28,
    227
  and Chinese noodles, 79, 227
  Chinese-style, 206
  croquettes with sweet potatoes, 140–41,
    190–91, 228
  in curried rice with raisins and almonds,
    131, 228
  curry, 97, 227
  with fried rice, 129
  and garlic, 49
  and gingered pea pods, 214
  gravy, 187
  hash, 35, 228
  in Japanese-style rolls with scallions, 31,
    228
  in lamejun, 101–3, 227
  leftover recipes for, 195, 196, 201, 205,
    207, 209, 210–11, 216–17, 220, 221–
    22
  in ma po dofu, 33, 227
  master recipe for, 186–87, 193
  and New Year's Eve stuffing, 188–90
  omelette, 211
  pancakes with potato and chives, 210–
    11
  pâté, 186, 205
  pot pie, 224–25
  roast, 186–87
  in sandwiches, 22–23, 207, 208, 227
  with sauce, 169, 218, 219, 221–22,
    228
  and sesame-chile noodles, 209
  in soups/stews, 195, 198
  stir-fried, 30, 122, 212–13, 227
  and sweet potatoes, 141
  tonnato, 216–17
  tortillas with bean salad, 217
  Vermont-Mex casserole, 220
Turkey—in salads
  bean and cilantro, 228, 255
  Chinese-style, 206
  with grapes, raisins and almonds in a
    chutney mayonnaise, 201
  lentil and rosemary, 203
  pasta, feta cheese and tomatoes, 205
  with sesame-chile noodles, 109
  with tuna, 216–17
Turkey stock, 50, 193, 195, 196, 221–22,
  224–25
Turnips, 14–15

Veal
  braised with vegetables, 243–44
  and celery remoulade with peppers, 28,
    250
  leftover recipes for, 245–50
  master recipe for, 243–44
  parsley and pine nuts stuffed mushrooms,
    110–11, 250
  in red wine, mushroom and cream sauce,
    34, 250
  with rotelle, zucchini and peppers, 248
  in sandwiches, 21, 250
  and spinach stuffed mushrooms, 249–50
  stir-fried, 107, 250
  tonnato, 216–17, 250
  with wild mushroom, tarragon and cream
    sauce, 221–22, 250
Veal—in salads
  with asparagus, 26, 250
  with asparagus and olives, 246
  with a green sauce, 245
  with horseradish sauce, 28–29, 250
  with oranges and tomatoes on a bed of
    spinach, 247
  with peppers and anchovy vinaigrette,
    68, 250
  potato salad with horseradish vinaigrette,
    25, 250
Veal stock, 154–55, 243–44
Vegetables
  and artichoke sauce, 261
  with braised veal, 243–44
  in chicken tortillas with bean salad, 217,
    263
  in chowder with lamb, leeks, and
    potatoes, 93, 263
  in croquettes with sweet potatoes, 140–41
  in fried rice, 130–31, 263
  and garlic, 49
  idea for leftover, 261
  with lamb shoulder, 88–89, 263
  marinade for, 262
  in omelettes, 121
  with pasta, 262
  in pasta frittata, 119
  with pasta of gratin, 117
  and peppers frittata, 259
  in pizza, 262, 263, 264
  in potato frittata, 142, 263
  in quiche, 175–76, 263
  in sandwiches, 262
  with sauces, 262
  in soups/stews, 154–55, 157, 197, 263
  stir-fried, 30, 77, 122, 212–13, 262

Vegetables (cont.)
  in tarts with salmon, spinach, and
    asparagus, 80–81, 263
  See also name of specific type of
    vegetable
Vegetables—in salads
  lentil and rosemary with duck, 203, 263
  pasta with asparagus, feta cheese, tomato
    and dill, 118
  pork and bean, 158, 263
  pork with mustard and soy sauce, 161
  potato, 139, 263
  spring steak and asparagus, 26, 263
Vinaigrette
  anchovy, 68
  artichoke heart and avocado, 256
  for Chinese pork and cabbage salad, 162
  cumin and mint, 158
  green, 235
  horseradish, 25
  lemon-basil, 160–61
  mustard and soy, 161
  orange/orange-flavored, 66, 247
  parmesan cheese in, 159, 160–61
  pepper and cornichon, 26
  scallions in, 25, 26, 256
  tahini-chile, 128
  tomatoes in, 256
  See also Lemons/lemon juice—in
    vinaigrette; Mustard—in vinaigrette
Vinegar, as a basic ingredient, 8

Walnuts, 19, 128, 200–201, 203, 262
Wasabi, 32
Water chestnuts, 95, 128
White beans. See Cannellini beans
White sauce, 104–5
Wine, as a basic ingredient, 8
Worchestershire sauce, 3

Yams, 134
Yogurt, 96, 98–99, 158, 222–23, 234–35,
    240, 246, 262
Yorkshire-style pudding, 38

Zucchini
  bread pudding, 45
  and ham and cream sauce, 170
  omelette with turkey and gouda cheese,
    211
  with pasta, veal, zucchini and peppers, 248
  in pasta e fagioli, 153
  in pizza, 264
  in potato frittata, 142